Mrs Hinch

THE ACTIVITY JOURNAL

*Relax Your Mind –
It's Time to Unwind*

MICHAEL JOSEPH

an imprint of

PENGUIN BOOKS

MICHAEL JOSEPH

UK | USA | Canada | Ireland | Australia
India | New Zealand | South Africa

Michael Joseph is part of the Penguin Random House group of companies
whose addresses can be found at global.penguinrandomhouse.com

First published 2019
001

Copyright © Mrs Hinch 2019

The moral right of the author has been asserted

Set in 12/15 Archer
Designed and typeset by Smith & Gilmour

Illustrations on pages 43, 44, 116, 187 © Alice Tait
Illustrations on pages 185 and 193 of Mrs Hinch by May van Millingen, based
on the original © Jane Sherburn, Golley Slater and Procter and Gamble UK Ltd
Illustration on page 169 of 'The Cloth Family' by May van Millingen,
based on the original artwork by Faye Finney, 2019
Illustrations on pages 3, 4, 16, 17, 19, 20, 21, 23, 27, 29, 32–33, 34, 36, 47, 58–59, 68, 70, 72–73,
80, 83, 91, 92, 93, 94, 97, 104–105, 115, 122, 135, 144–145, 146, 148, 156–158, 173, 184–185, 186, 193,
194–195, 210–211, 219, 220–221, 243, 245, 246, 255, 256–8, 266–267, 268 © May van Millingen, 2019
Illustrations on pages 56, 60, 96, 159, 172, 231, 244 © Emily Wallace, 2019
Illustrations on pages 37, 85, 109, 130, 137, 163, 237, 259, 271, 274 © Andy Smith, 2019
Illustrations on pages 10–11, 12–15, 22, 30–31, 46, 55, 57, 61, 67, 71, 80–81, 82, 83, 84, 106–107, 108,
118–119, 120–121, 129, 132, 136, 146–7, 160–161, 174–175, 197, 209, 213, 234–235, 247 © Shutterstock
Additional illustrations Smith & Gilmour
*Every effort has been made to trace copyright holders and obtain permission
for the use of copyright material. If any omission or error has been made
please notify the publisher for correction in future editions.*

Printed in Germany by GGP Media GmbH, Poessneck

A CIP catalogue record for this book is available from the British Library

ISBN: 978–0–241–42684–5

www.greenpenguin.co.uk

Penguin Random House is committed to a
sustainable future for our business, our readers
and our planet. This book is made from Forest
Stewardship Council® certified paper.

Mrs Hinch

THE ACTIVITY
JOURNAL

To My Amazing Hincher

Mrs Hinch here!
I want to welcome you personally to *your* journal.
It might have my name on it, but this book is all for you.

So many of you have told me how much hinching helps you. You've told me that it helps you clear your mind and makes you feel more positive. One of the things that I've learnt since starting my Instagram account is how many of us all feel the same way. I can honestly say that I never realised! I always thought I was on my own, but your love and support has genuinely blown me away, and we really are all in this together!

Why I Wrote This Book

This got me thinking about some of the other things that I do to feel better. Those little things, some of which you've seen me have a go at, to try and help relax my mind and unwind. You know the feeling that you get after you stand back and admire your freshly hinched bathroom? Or how satisfied you feel after you've managed to tick everything off your hinch list? That is how I'd like us all to feel after we've spent a few minutes, or even half an hour each day, taking some time out for ourselves, completing our books. I want this book to make us smile, to make us feel motivated, and to make us feel happy. And I want us to all have a laugh together.

You all mean the absolute world to me. You've changed my life! Without you I would never have known that there are so many people out there who feel just like I do! When you tell me how much my stories and hinching make you smile and brighten up your day, it melts my heart! You've all helped me so much that I really wanted to do something for you.

What's In This Activity Journal?

A lot of the time when we have our chats through DMs and when we've met each other in person, you tell me all about how busy your lives are and how stressful it is trying to balance everything you have going on. It makes me happier than I can ever tell you that watching my stories gives you a little break in your really busy day. A break to just sit down and relax for a few moments with a cup of tea and me and my crazy little Hinch family life. What I wanted from this book was to give us all more reasons to have a sit down and find an excuse to take some me-time. Making time for ourselves is so important!

Inside, you'll find loads of fun, silly Hinch-themed activities to complete as a way to unwind and de-stress, as well as more thoughtful pages to write down how you feel, and to reflect on how your week has been. You all know exactly how I feel about being organised, so I've made sure to include loads of planning pages. Planning pages for your home, but also planning pages for your mind, your goals, your dreams. And it wouldn't be a book about Mrs Hinch without checklists, now, would it, so there are plenty of those!

So grab your highlighters and your crystal pens, Hinchers, and let's get cracking!

Using This Activity Journal

This book is all yours, to use exactly as you'd like! There are absolutely no rules here! You know how I just like to wing it! You can start it whenever you feel like it, and on whatever page you'd prefer.

♡

You will see in the next couple of pages I have filled out an example hinch list, showing you the sorts of things I like to write when I'm planning my to-dos. I absolutely love a hinch list, so I thought we could start every week with one. There is no better way of getting things I need to do out of my head and on to the page. And I find I'm much more likely to actually get on and do things if I write them down. I've also included some notes pages and some tadaa lists for you to fill out at the back. Tadaa lists are for those days when a to-do list just seems a bit too much. A tadaa list is basically like a backwards hinch list, where you write down things you have already achieved. I thought it would be nice for us to be able to reflect on how our week has been, so I've also included a journal page at the end of every week. You will see my example journal page, where I have filled out my journal for that week, so you can see the sorts of things I include. I really hope you enjoy!

♡

The idea is that you try to make completing this activity journal a part of your daily routine. Set aside some time, hopefully every day, but if not every day then whenever you can, to take some dedicated time out, to relax and unwind with the help of the activities in this book.

♡

I hope that this book will also help you to figure out which activities work in helping you to relax too. And that the puzzles and games put a big smile on your face.

♡

Most of all, I hope you can take a bit of time out, curl up in your comfy spot with your book and feel settled and cosy and safe. You deserve it.

♡

MY WEEKLY HINCH LIST

HALLWAY AND LANDING

- Doors + woodwork ✓
- Space tidy baskets ✓
- Carpet Fresh + hoover ☐
- Shine ornaments ✓
- Front door mat ☐
- Vera floors ✓
- ☐
- ☐
- ☐

BATHROOM

- Wipe & pine toilet ✓
- Shower screen ☐
- Plugs ☐
- Tiles ✓
- Bath and taps ☐
- ☐
- ☐
- ☐
- ☐

HENRY'S ROOM

- Carpet Fresh + hoover ✓
- Dave + Sheen ✓
- Fold clothes + put away ✓
- Change bed sheets ✓
- Dettol sheets ✓
- ☐
- ☐
- ☐
- ☐

KITCHEN

- Microwave ✓
- Shine the sink ✓
- Plugholes ☐
- Check/chuck fridge food ☐
- Stock check hinching baskets ☐
- ☐
- ☐
- ☐
- ☐

A typical example of my hinch list!

LOUNGE

TV screen	✓
Dave + Sheen	☐
Hoover and Vera the floor	✓
Mirrors	☐
Windows	☐
Remote controls	✓
	☐
	☐
	☐

ODD JOBS

Labels for new baskets	✓
Henry groomers	☐
Blow dry	☐
	☐
	☐

AD-HOC

Oven filter	☐
Lanterns	✓
Empty laundry basket	☐
	☐

ME-TIME

X Factor and	☐
takeaway on Friday	☐
Get nails done	✓
	☐
	☐
	☐
	☐
	☐

HINCH HAUL

SHOPPING LIST

Milk	☐
Special K	☐
Bananas	☐
Nappies	☐
Zoflora	☐
	☐
	☐
	☐
	☐

MY JOURNAL

Date: Sunday 23rd

Three things I'm proud I accomplished this week:

1 >> Ronnie's injections because, let's face it, they're awful! But it had to be done! I'd been dreading it for weeks and I feel a huge relief now that it's over.

2 >> I bought my mum and dad their dream patio garden set, bless them. They are so over the moon with it, it made my heart melt! Dad loves to dust it down every night before bed and put the chairs away nicely! Simple things really are the best.

3 >> This may sound like a silly accomplishment to some people but for me it's quite a big deal. I went out on my own with Ronnie and Henry to the park for the first time. I normally go with Jamie or my mum but this time I went alone and I felt in control for the first time in a long time. I even managed to keep calm when Ronnie started crying at the same time Henry was barking at the young lads playing football! I felt proud of myself when I got home.

What was the best day of the week and why? TUESDAY! Jamie's family came to visit! They are the most amazing people. We may not see Jamie's family as much as we see mine because distance can be a bugger but when we are together it's just perfect. I'm so pleased Ronnie has such a strong family that love him to pieces.

What was the most challenging day of the week and why? Definitely Ronnie's immunisation jabs! I felt terrible afterwards because he really cried and I didn't want him to be in pain. The nurse reassured me that a lot of parents feel this way so I'm not alone on this one!

This week I was inspired by: There was a couple on This Morning that had been married for 80 years! Yep, 80 whole years! And they still looked so in love, and the way the husband looked at his wife when she laughed was beautiful. Now that really is inspirational! I hope Jamie still looks at me that way 80 years down the line, haha!

If I could relive any moment from this week, which one would it be and why? Thursday morning! Me, Jamie, Henry and Ronnie were all together in the bed laughing and just taking everything in around us. Because our lives really have changed since Ronnie arrived (for the better) and sometimes it's nice to just reflect and talk things through, isn't it?

Favourite quote of the week: Be strong now because things will get better; it might be stormy now but it can't rain forever.

Favourite thing I hinched this week: My sink, Ronnie's wardrobe and the fridge.

Three things to look forward to next week:

- Spending time in the garden
- Trying a new recipe
- Going out with Jamie and Ronnie and Henry on a walk to our local woods

A typical example of my journal!

All About YOU

First I'm going to tell you a little bit more about me.
Then I'd love to get to know you better!

Name: Sophie Hinchliffe

Birthday: 16th February   Age: 29   Star sign: Aquarius

My family: Husband Jamie, Baby Ronnie and Fur Baby Henry
(my Handsomes)

Describe yourself in three words: Determined, Worrier,
Beyoncé-obsessed (oh wait, that's four!)

What quality do you like most about yourself? My determination
to help others

Write something unique about you that not many people would know:
I love to sing and I haven't got a bad singing voice either!

What do you like to do in your spare time? Hinch!

If you could have one wish come true, what would it be? For everything
to stay exactly how it is now, forever...

Favourite line from a movie: If you can't say something nice, don't
say nothing at all – Bambi

If you were to be well-known, what would it be for? Pine-ing my loo and shining my sink, apparently! Haha!

Favourite animal: Dogs – aka Handsomes

Favourite meal: My mum's roast dinner!

If you could have a super power, what would it be? To enable us to all live life twice

Name one thing you can't live without: Jamie

Favourite colour: Grey all the way!

Favourite saying: All the best!

Favourite season: Autumn

Favourite TV programme/movie: The Pursuit of Happyness

Favourite book: Hinch Yourself Happy

Favourite singer/group: Beyoncé

Person you find most inspiring: My dad

Favourite place to go on holiday: The Maldives

Favourite room in your house: Kitchen

Favourite hinch: Hoovering with Sharon!

Favourite quote: Never regret being a good person to the wrong people! Your kindness says everything about you. Their behaviour says everything about them.

NOW IT'S YOUR TURN

Name: ....

Birthday: .... Age: .... Star sign: ....

My family: ....

....

Describe yourself in three words: ....

What quality do you like most about yourself? ....

....

....

Write something unique about you that not many people would know:

....

....

What do you like to do in your spare time? ....

If you could have one wish come true, what would it be? ....

....

Favourite line from a movie: ....

....

If you were to be well-known, what would it be for?

Favourite animal:

Favourite meal:

If you could have a super power, what would it be?

Name one thing you can't live without:

Favourite colour:

Favourite saying:

Favourite season:

Favourite TV programme/movie:

Favourite book:

Favourite singer/group:

Person you find most inspiring:

Favourite place to go on holiday:

Favourite room in your house:

Favourite hinch:

Favourite quote:

Goals are dreams
with a guide.

However big your life goals are, I hope you
believe me when I say: you've got this.

Alongside giving you space to relax and unwind, I really want this book to give you the space to dream and plan. So please list your top three goals below. Remember, dream big! You can achieve anything you put your mind to. I genuinely believe that, Hinchers! You will come back to these three goals later in the book, so have a think about the three things you most want to achieve. And don't worry if this seems a bit much to start off with. Feel free to revisit these goal-setting pages whenever you feel ready!

1»

2»

3»

We'll take a look at your goals in-depth over the next few pages.

How To Achieve Your Goals

Look at the goals on your list. Do they sound overwhelming and unreachable? What I've found is that you can make your hopes and dreams come true by coming up with a plan! Take baby steps in approaching your goals and break them down into manageable parts with the help of this guide.

What will you do in the next week?

What will you do in the next month?

What will you do in the next three months?

What will you do in the next six months?

What will you do in the next year?

You can use this list every week, to keep checking in with your journey towards your goal. All the best!

☐ My goal » ....

☐ In the next week » ....
....
....

☐ In the next month » ....
....
....

☐ In the next three months » ....
....
....

☐ In the next six months » ....
....
....

☐ In the next year » ....
....
....

When you have completed each part of your goal, tick the box!

☐ My goal » ....

☐ In the next week » ....
....
....

☐ In the next month » ....
....
....

☐ In the next three months » ....
....
....

☐ In the next six months » ....
....
....

☐ In the next year » ....
....
....

When you have completed each part of your goal, tick the box!

☐ My goal » ....

☐ In the next week » ....

....

....

☐ In the next month » ....

....

....

☐ In the next three months » ....

....

....

☐ In the next six months » ....

....

....

☐ In the next year » ....

....

....

When you have completed each part of your goal, tick the box!

I hope you have
a wonderful day,
my Hincher!

Love from me,
Soph xxx

LET'S GET STARTED!

MY WEEKLY HINCH LIST

- [ ] ....
- [ ] ....
- [ ] ....
- [ ] ....
- [ ] ....
- [ ] ....
- [ ] ....
- [ ] ....
- [ ] ....

- [ ] ....
- [ ] ....
- [ ] ....
- [ ] ....
- [ ] ....
- [ ] ....
- [ ] ....
- [ ] ....
- [ ] ....

- [ ] ....
- [ ] ....
- [ ] ....
- [ ] ....
- [ ] ....
- [ ] ....
- [ ] ....
- [ ] ....
- [ ] ....

- [ ] ....
- [ ] ....
- [ ] ....
- [ ] ....
- [ ] ....
- [ ] ....
- [ ] ....
- [ ] ....
- [ ] ....

HINCH LIST *continued*

- [ ] ....
- [ ] ....
- [ ] ....
- [ ] ....
- [ ] ....
- [ ] ....
- [ ] ....
- [ ] ....

- [ ] ....
- [ ] ....
- [ ] ....
- [ ] ....
- [ ] ....
- [ ] ....
- [ ] ....
- [ ] ....

HINCH HAUL

- [ ] ....
- [ ] ....
- [ ] ....
- [ ] ....
- [ ] ....
- [ ] ....
- [ ] ....
- [ ] ....
- [ ] ....

- [ ] ....
- [ ] ....
- [ ] ....
- [ ] ....
- [ ] ....
- [ ] ....
- [ ] ....
- [ ] ....
- [ ] ....

I'd love to see your hinch lists!

#mrshinchtheactivityjournal

Hinchionary Word Search

Can you spot some of our favourite words and sayings?

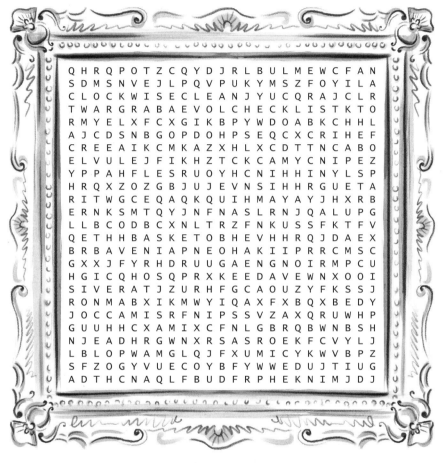

```
Q H R Q P O T Z C Q Y D J R L B U L M E W C F A N
S D M S N V E J L P Q V P U K Y M S Z F O Y I L A
C L O C K W I S E C L E A N J Y U C Q R A J C L R
T W A R G R A B A E V O L C H E C K L I S T K T O
R M Y E L X F C X G I K B P Y W D O A B K C H H L
A J C D S N B G O P D O H P S E Q C X C R I H E F
C R E E A I K C M K A Z X H L X C D T T N C A B O
E L V U L E J F I K H Z T C K C A M Y C N I P E Z
Y P P A H F L E S R U O Y H C N I H H I N Y L S P
H R Q X Z O Z G B J U J E V N S I H H R G U E T A
R I T W G C E Q A Q K Q U I H M A Y A Y J H X R B
E R N K S M T Q Y J N F N A S L R N J Q A L U P G
L L B C O D B C X N L T R Z F N K U S S F K T F V
Q E T H H B A S K E T O B H E V H H R Q J D A E X
B R B A V E N I A P N E O H A K I I P R R C M S C
G X X J F Y R H D R U U G A E N G N O I R M P C U
H G I C Q H O S Q P R X K E E D A V E W N X O O I
S I V E R A T J Z U R H F G C A O U Z Y F K S S J
R O N M A B X I K M W Y I Q A X F X B Q X B E D Y
J O C C A M I S R F N I P S S V Z A X Q R U W H P
G U U H H C X A M I X C F N L G B R Q B W N B S H
N J E A D H R G W N X R S A S R O E K F C V Y L J
L B L O P W A M G L Q J F X U M I C Y K W V B P Z
S F Z O G Y V U E C O Y B F Y W W E D U J T I U G
A D T H C N A Q L F B U D F R P H E K N I M J D J
```

- ☐ All The Best
- ☐ Love A Barg
- ☐ Narnia
- ☐ Hinch Haul
- ☐ Vera
- ☐ Zoflora
- ☐ Basket
- ☐ Shine
- ☐ Fur Baby
- ☐ Checklist
- ☐ Hinch Half Hour
- ☐ Clockwise Clean
- ☐ Pinkeh
- ☐ Henry Hinch
- ☐ Home
- ☐ Minkeh
- ☐ Grey
- ☐ Hinchers
- ☐ Trace
- ☐ Dave
- ☐ Sharon
- ☐ Hinch Yourself Happy

Answers on page 282

Be Kind To Yourself

I want to start by saying that you are perfect exactly the way you are. I know how easy it is for us to judge ourselves, and how hard it can be to notice our good points. We don't want to build ourselves up in case we are knocked down.

Well, this might feel a bit cringe but now I'm going to ask you to list your good points. As you write them down, I hope you'll start to really believe them. I'm not talking about how you look – this is all about the lovely and amazing person I know you are on the inside. I'll start, so you don't feel embarrassed!

So, some of the things I would put for me are:

KIND	POSITIVE	FUN
FUNNY	TIDY	CARING
LOYAL	FRIENDLY	LOVING
HELPFUL	SILLY	

If you find it hard, use this trick: think what your friends and family would say about you.

Draw yourself here

(Don't worry, it doesn't have to be a work of art – I can't draw to save my life!)

Which kind words would you use to describe yourself?

....

....

....

....

My Top 10 Hinching Must-Haves

You know I have my favourites that I can't hinch without! But you Hinchers have also told me all about the products you love too. I'm going to tell you my top 10 and then I'd love for you to tell me yours!

MY TOP 10 PRODUCTS (*in no particular order*):

1 » Zoflora (I'm drawing the line at picking just one favourite scent! Haha!)

2 » Febreze

3 » Elbow Grease De-Greaser

4 » Flash Bathroom Spray

5 » Harpic Active Fresh Mountain Pine

6 » Cliff the Cif Perfect Finish Stainless Steel Cleaner Spray

7 » The Pink Stuff

8 » Dettol Disinfectant Spray

9 » Cif Wipes

10 » Mr Sheen Multi-Surface Original Polish

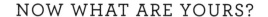

NOW WHAT ARE YOURS?

1 »

2 »

3 »

4 »

5 »

6 »

7 »

8 »

9 »

10 »

Honestly, this was tricky for me!
It's like being asked to pick
your favourite child!

Sophie's Kitchen

This room is easily my favourite place in the whole house! Colour it in and don't forget to share and #mrshinchtheactivityjournal

A Calm, Cosy Corner

I've always been very open about the fact that I'm a worrier. My home has always been my safe space; the place where my mind feels most at rest. I thought it would be an amazing idea for us all to create a dedicated calm corner in our homes. Somewhere we all know we can go, just to take a few moments to breathe and gather our thoughts, when we need to. If your house is often full of people, where can you go to escape? I'd like you to think of a place in your home and create a cosy corner where you can just chill. It doesn't matter how big or how small. This is your space. It might be an armchair or the corner of a sofa. Or it might be a cushion on the floor with a view of the garden, even. Collect some things to make it even cosier. You know how I can't resist a fleece blanket and some cushions! I would also have some candles and my favourite wax melt on the go in mine, because smells are such a strong soother for me.

Try to spend a few minutes every day in your calm corner. Sit with your eyes closed and relax your mind, slowly breathing in and out.

The idea is that thinking of nothing for a while is good for you and helps to keep you calm.

DESCRIBE YOUR OWN PERFECT CALM SPACE:

Zoflora
Where It All Began

Zoflora is one of my absolute must-have products. I couldn't be without it! I love it so much that I have a dedicated hour every so often where I'll visit their website and blitz the house room by room using just Zoflora. It leaves the house smelling amazing! I don't think you'll believe just how many Zoflora scents there have been, past and present. There are over 40 fragrances, Hinchers! List as many as you can think of here, and then label the bottles with your top three faves!

Answers on page 282

No one is **you** and that is your **POWER**

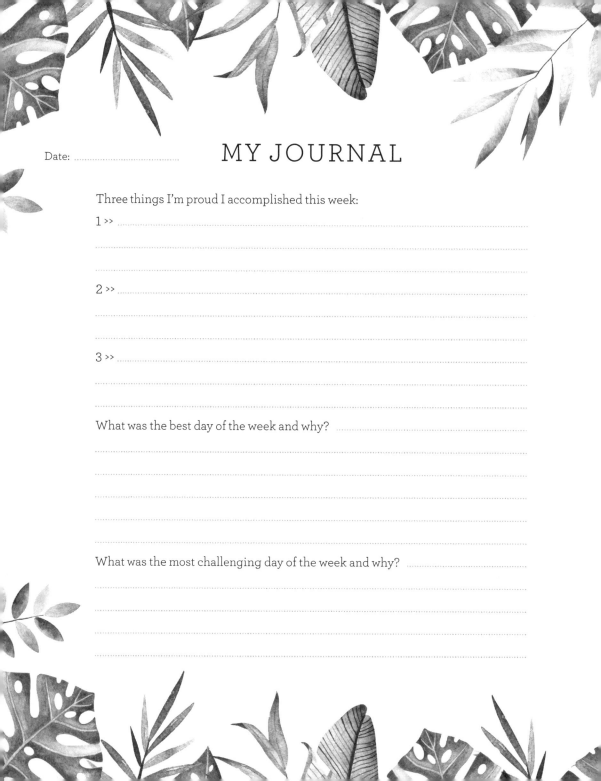

MY JOURNAL

Date: ....

Three things I'm proud I accomplished this week:

1 >> ....

....

....

2 >> ....

....

....

3 >> ....

....

....

What was the best day of the week and why? ....

....

....

....

....

What was the most challenging day of the week and why? ....

....

....

....

This week I was inspired by: ....
....
....

If I could relive any moment from this week, which one would it be and why?
....
....
....
....

Favourite quote of the week: ....
....
....
....

Favourite thing I hinched this week: ....
....
....
....

Three things to look forward to next week:
♥ ....
....
♥ ....
....
♥ ....
....

Date: ....

MY WEEKLY HINCH LIST

- [ ]
- [ ]
- [ ]
- [ ]
- [ ]
- [ ]
- [ ]
- [ ]
- [ ]

- [ ]
- [ ]
- [ ]
- [ ]
- [ ]
- [ ]
- [ ]
- [ ]

- [ ]
- [ ]
- [ ]
- [ ]
- [ ]
- [ ]
- [ ]
- [ ]
- [ ]

- [ ]
- [ ]
- [ ]
- [ ]
- [ ]
- [ ]
- [ ]
- [ ]

HINCH LIST *continued*

- [ ]
- [ ]
- [ ]
- [ ]
- [ ]
- [ ]
- [ ]
- [ ]
- [ ]

- [ ]
- [ ]
- [ ]
- [ ]
- [ ]
- [ ]
- [ ]
- [ ]
- [ ]

- [ ]
- [ ]
- [ ]
- [ ]
- [ ]
- [ ]
- [ ]
- [ ]
- [ ]

HINCH HAUL

- [ ]
- [ ]
- [ ]
- [ ]
- [ ]
- [ ]
- [ ]
- [ ]
- [ ]

Finding The Hinching Names

Draw lines to match each product with its hinching family name

Barry	antibacterial cleaning pad
Buff Tings	brushes
Clarence	Dishmatic
Cliff	fluffy duster
Dave	glass and window cloth
Derek	gloves
Gregory	kneeling pad
Kermit	lint roller
Lennie	mop slippers
Minkeh	moppet sponge
Neil	polish cloth
Pinkeh	sonic scrubber
Sharon	spray mop
Stewart	stainless-steel spray
Trace	turbo mop
Vera	vacuum cleaner
Victor	window vacuum

Answers on page 282

Count Your Blessings

Sometimes when I feel like the worrying and nervous tummy are getting on top of me, I like to sit down and do this little exercise and it makes me feel so much better. It's one of the main ways I remind myself just how blessed and fortunate I am, and how much I love my normal life.

It was my mum who taught me to count my blessings. I truly believe that we live our happiest and best lives when we learn to appreciate the simple things around us. Doing this little task every day will really help to show you that you have so much to be grateful for right under your nose.

HOW TO DO IT:
Write down five things you are grateful for. They can be things you're happy to have in your life, something amazing that happened that day, or the people who you love, who make you laugh, or who make you feel safe. They can be really big things, like your home, down to the smallest of things, like your friends popping by for a cuppa, or your mum's cracking Sunday roast dinner.

THESE ARE MY BLESSINGS, RIGHT NOW:

1. My boys: Jamie, Ronnie and Henry Hinch … my Handsomes.

2. My family and best friends, especially my mum. She is my everything.

3. My Hinchers. (You all know who you are!)

4. My health, because without that where would I be? I feel so blessed!

5. The ability to grow my home. People have said to me, 'Soph, why don't you move to a new, bigger house?' and I think to myself, 'Why? I love my home!' So as my family has grown, I've grown my home.

NOW LIST SOME OF YOURS:

1. ....

2. ....

3. ....

4. ....

5. ....

3 MORE WAYS TO BE THANKFUL

1

Decide to say 'thank you' more. It might be for a big thing or just a small one, but when you say it, really mean it. It makes other people happy and it will make you happy too.

2

When you're done hinching a room and you've ticked off your hinch list, stop for a minute. Make sure you take some time to look around and appreciate how clean and fresh everything is, and take in the shine.

3

Live in the moment and be grateful for what you have in that second. The more you do this, the more the habit will form and the easier it will be.

The Category Challenge

Fill in the blanks with words that begin with the letter

H

Shop name	
Author	
Celebrity	
Cleaning product	
Flower	
Car model	
Dog breed	
Country	
Item of clothing	
Fruit	
Insect	
Something cold	
Body part	
Animal	
Household item	
Hobby	
Spice or herb	
Restaurant	
Occupation	
Something that makes you smile	

Where's Minkeh?

Our main man is hiding somewhere in this magical Narnia – can you spot him?

Colour in Narnia

Answer on page 283

Happiness Wheel

Now, I know exactly what you're thinking ... We haven't come here to do maths homework, Soph! I can't say I was ever great at graphs and charts myself, but this activity is a bit of a different way to help us focus on all the things we love in our lives. I've filled in eighteen of my favourite things and there's a blank wheel opposite for you to do the same.

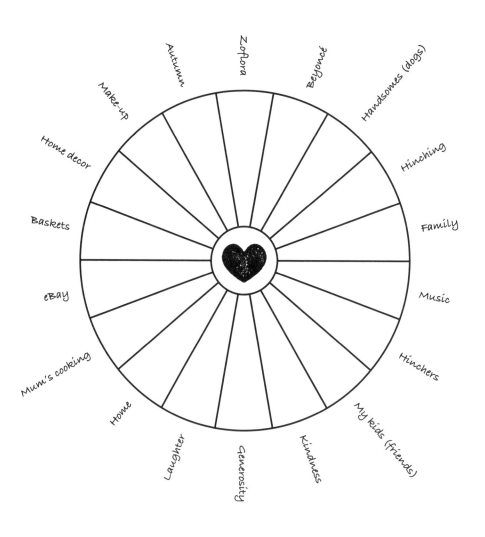

Don't forget to colour the sections in when you're done!
Any excuse to get the colouring pens out!

Here's yours to complete:

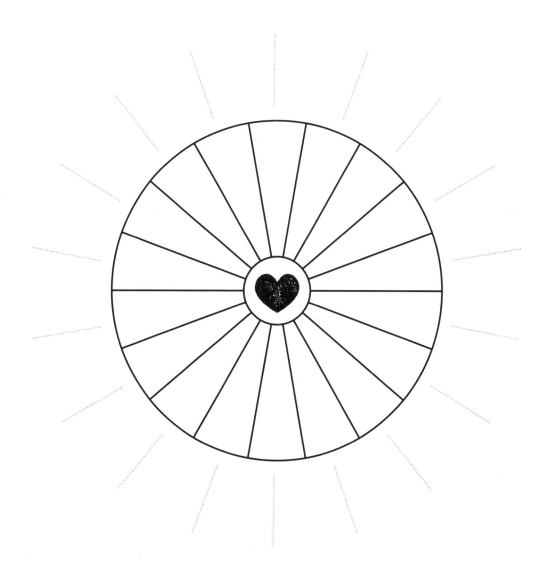

Date: ....

MY JOURNAL

Three things I'm proud I accomplished this week:

1 >> ....

....

....

2 >> ....

....

....

3 >> ....

....

....

What was the best day of the week and why? ....

....

....

....

....

What was the most challenging day of the week and why? ....

....

....

....

....

This week I was inspired by: ....

....

If I could relive any moment from this week, which one would it be and why?

....

....

....

Favourite quote of the week: ....

....

....

Favourite thing I hinched this week: ....

....

....

Three things to look forward to next week:

♥ ....

....

♥ ....

....

♥ ....

....

Date: ....

MY WEEKLY HINCH LIST

HINCH LIST *continued*

☐
☐
☐
☐
☐
☐
☐
☐
☐

☐
☐
☐
☐
☐
☐
☐
☐
☐

HINCH HAUL

☐
☐
☐
☐
☐
☐
☐
☐
☐

☐
☐
☐
☐
☐
☐
☐
☐
☐

Don't forget to share your hinch lists!

#mrshinchtheactivityjournal

Start Your Own Hinching Playlist

Music makes me so happy and, as I'm sure you've seen on my stories, it really helps me get into the rhythm of things when I hinch! If you choose the right tune, you can sing along to it and it really gets you going and gives you that extra bit of motivation! To help get you started with your playlist, I've listed my top five tracks.

SOME OF MY FAVE SONGS TO HINCH TO:

★ Marvin Gaye and Tammi Terrell – 'Ain't No Mountain High Enough'

★ Beyoncé – 'I Was Here'

★ Usher – 'U Got It Bad'

★ Blinkie – 'Don't Give Up (On Love)'

★ Miguel – 'Pineapple Skies'

Now start filling in yours, and you'll be on your way to making a banging list of tunes to hinch to!

★ ....

★ ....

★ ....

★ ....

★ ....

DOT-TO-DOT

Don't forget to colour me in afterwards!

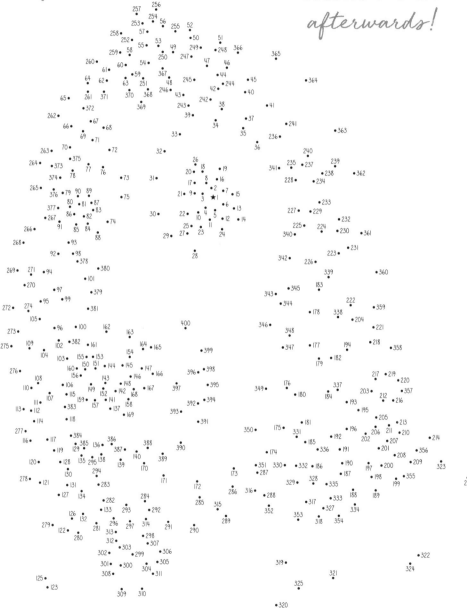

Answers on page 283

TV SHOWS
THIS *or* THAT

Underline your fave from each pair!

Love Island ⟷ I'm a Celebrity…

The Great British Bake Off ⟷ MasterChef

This Morning ⟷ BBC Breakfast

Keeping Up with the Kardashians ⟷ The Real Housewives

EastEnders ⟷ Coronation Street

Garden Rescue ⟷ Homes Under the Hammer

Made in Chelsea ⟷ TOWIE

The Apprentice ⟷ Dragons' Den

Antiques Roadshow ⟷ Bargain Hunt

The Voice ⟷ Britain's Got Talent

Friends ⟷ Modern Family

Wimbledon ⟷ FIFA World Cup

Home Improvements On A Barg

There are so, so many ways to give your home a new lease of life without having to spend a lot! I live for a barg, and I love upcycling old pieces – or even changing new, inexpensive pieces to make them unique and give them a little something extra. I get so many questions about the box shelves in my kitchen, and they're only from IKEA! I painted them grey and distressed them a little, and to me they look perf! Exactly what I wanted! Changing the big stuff can be so expensive, so I wanted us to use these little frames to plan out any little (or big, if you like – no rules here, remember!) improvements that we could make to the rooms or items of furniture in our homes. You'll be amazed at what a difference something as little as changing your kitchen-cabinet door handles can make. Trust me, and try it!

Doodle Me!

Doodling is a great way to tap into your arty side and get creative. It's also a really great way to relax. I've said before, I'm certainly no artist, but I enjoy getting all my pens out and having a go. Let's all use this page to do the same!

Just do your best and
realise that is enough.
Don't compare
yourself to anyone.
Be happy to be the
wonderful, unique, very
special person that you are
– Susan Polis Schutz

MY JOURNAL

Date: ....

Three things I'm proud I accomplished this week:

1 >> ....

....

....

2 >> ....

....

....

3 >> ....

....

....

What was the best day of the week and why? ....

....

....

....

....

What was the most challenging day of the week and why? ....

....

....

....

....

This week I was inspired by: ....

....

....

If I could relive any moment from this week, which one would it be and why?

....

....

....

....

Favourite quote of the week: ....

....

....

....

Favourite thing I hinched this week: ....

....

....

....

Three things to look forward to next week:

♥ ....

....

♥ ....

....

♥ ....

....

Date: ....

MY WEEKLY HINCH LIST

HINCH HAUL

Sudoku Fun

Fill in the missing squares!

HINCH HINT: Each large square must contain the numbers 1 to 9. Each column and row must also contain the numbers 1 to 9.

3			4				1	
					9	8		2
		8	6				3	
4	5							9
	2			7				
	3		2			5	6	
	1	3	8					7
5		7			2			3
		2	7		3		9	

Answers on page 283

Home is where my heart is!

What Home Means To Me

As soon as I open my front door, I can feel my worries start to melt away. It is my sanctuary – the place I feel most calm. As I've said before, home is where my heart is.

That's why I spend so much time making my house into a home, hinching it and loving it. Yours doesn't have to be spotless, or perfect, or like anyone else's. To be a home, it just needs to be a place that makes you feel comfortable and safe.

3 THINGS THAT MAKE MY HOUSE A HOME:

1 » Home is … karate-chopped cushions and belly baskets.

2 » Home is … the familiar scent of Zoflora and my favourite wax melts, and a freshly pined loo.

3 » Home is … wherever Jamie, Ronnie and Henry are.

WHAT HOME MEANS TO YOU:

1» Home is...

2» Home is...

3» Home is...

4» Home is...

5» Home is...

How quickly can you unscramble these Hincher favourites?
Fill in the blanks with the unscrambled words.

1. furl hora zoo

_ _ _ _ _ _ _ / _ _ _ _

HINT: The most fragrant time of day!

2. bees ray

_ _ _ _ _ _ _

HINT: Some of my best purchases.

3. biff stung

_ _ _ _ / _ _ _ _ _

HINT: Essential hinching footwear.

4. flori hah hcuhn

_ _ _ _ _ / _ _ _ _ / _ _ _ _

HINT: One of my favourite cleaning routines.

5. knits puff

_ _ _ _ / _ _ _ _ _

HINT: You can always find this in my Narnia!

6. duvets earthed

_ _ _ _ / _ _ _ / _ _ _ _ _ _

HINT: Fluffy little guy.

7. hpnike

_ _ _ _ _ _

HINT: Amazing teamed with diluted Zoflora spray.

8. ins mekon think

_ _ _ _ / _ _ / _ _ _ / _ _ _ _

HINT: We had fun at Hinchmas time with this one.

9. amex pipits

_ _ _ _ _ / _ _ _ _ _

HINT: Looks amazing if you've got people coming to stay.

10. ballet seth

_ _ _ / _ _ _ / _ _ _ _

HINT: My number one catchphrase.

Answers on page 283

SOPHIE'S NACHOS

180g bag Cool Original
    Doritos
1 red onion
2 peppers
1 bottle sweet chilli sauce
Mature cheddar cheese
    (as much as you fancy)
1 pot sour cream

1. Preheat the oven to 150°C/gas mark 2.

2. Empty a full bag of Doritos into a large Pyrex dish and spread them out.

3. Chop up one red onion and two peppers and spread evenly all over the Doritos.

4. Pour an entire bottle of sweet chilli sauce over the contents of the Pyrex dish.

5. Sprinkle over as much grated cheese as you like.

6. Place in the oven and observe until golden.

7. Enjoy with a pot of sour cream.

It's no secret, I'm no Delia in the kitchen, but I love having a go. My nachos recipe is one of my faves. I've left some space for you below to write a recipe you're going to try in the next week. Don't forget to tag me, Hinchers! I would LOVE to try making one of your dishes too!

Grow Some Plant Power!

When I started growing herbs and plants in my garden, I didn't think I'd be able to keep them alive! I've killed so many houseplants! But Keith the Leaf is going strong! It really makes me happy to take care of my plants and watch them grow with all their new little leaves. If now isn't the right time for a fur baby in your life, why don't you consider getting yourself some plant babies to take care of?

Take some time to colour in
these lovely plants – the perfect
anti-stress activity!

MY JOURNAL

Date: ....

Three things I'm proud I accomplished this week:

1 >> ....
....
....

2 >> ....
....
....

3 >> ....
....
....

What was the best day of the week and why? ....
....
....
....
....

What was the most challenging day of the week and why? ....
....
....
....
....

This week I was inspired by: ....

....

If I could relive any moment from this week, which one would it be and why?

....

....

....

....

Favourite quote of the week: ....

....

....

....

Favourite thing I hinched this week: ....

....

....

....

Three things to look forward to next week:

♥ ....

....

♥ ....

....

♥ ....

....

Date: ....

MY WEEKLY HINCH LIST

HINCH LIST *continued*

☐
☐
☐
☐
☐
☐
☐
☐
☐

☐
☐
☐
☐
☐
☐
☐
☐
☐

HINCH HAUL

☐
☐
☐
☐
☐
☐
☐
☐
☐

☐
☐
☐
☐
☐
☐
☐
☐
☐

I'd love to see your hinch lists!

#mrshinchtheactivityjournal

CROSSWORD

ACROSS

1. Where did Mr Hinch and I have our first date?
4. How old was Handsomes Henry on his birthday in 2019?
5. Where did Mr Hinch and I go for our honeymoon?
7. What am I trained in workwise?
9. Where am I from?
11. What is the name of my first book?
17. What is my favourite scent of Ava May wax melts?
18. What does my mum do for a living?
19. Who is the cloth that started it all?
20. Who am I absolutely obsessed with?

DOWN

2. What is the notorious song associated with our Minkeh?
3. What football team does Mr Hinch support?
6. .... the Duster
8. What does ATB stand for?
10. On what programme did I make my first TV appearance?
12. What is my all-time favourite Zoflora if I was made to choose?
13. Hinch .... Hour
14. What do I call the cupboard where I keep all of my hinching products?
15. What hospital was I born in?
16. Which of my friends is one of my mops named after?

Answers on page 284

Dream Holiday

Who doesn't love a well-earned holiday? Whether it's a cosy staycation at home or jumping on a plane to an amazingly sunny exotic beach somewhere. Use these pages to dream about your ultimate holiday; and, if you've got one coming up, use this space to plan out your packing. Bon voyage, Hinchers!

FILL IN YOUR HOLIDAY PLANS HERE:

Where is your dream holiday destination? ....

....

Who would be your dream holiday buddy? ....

....

What are your holiday must-haves? ....

....

....

Write your packing list here. Don't forget your phone charger!

....

....

....

....

....

....

....

....

....

....

....

The Category Challenge

Fill in the blanks with words that begin with the letter

I

Shop name	....
Author	....
Celebrity	....
Cleaning product	....
Flower	....
Car model	....
Dog breed	....
Country	....
Item of clothing	....
Fruit	....
Insect	....
Something cold	....
Body part	....
Animal	....
Household item	....
Hobby	....
Spice or herb	....
Restaurant	....
Occupation	....
Something that makes you smile	....

Match The Hinching Product

Help me untangle my hinch list!

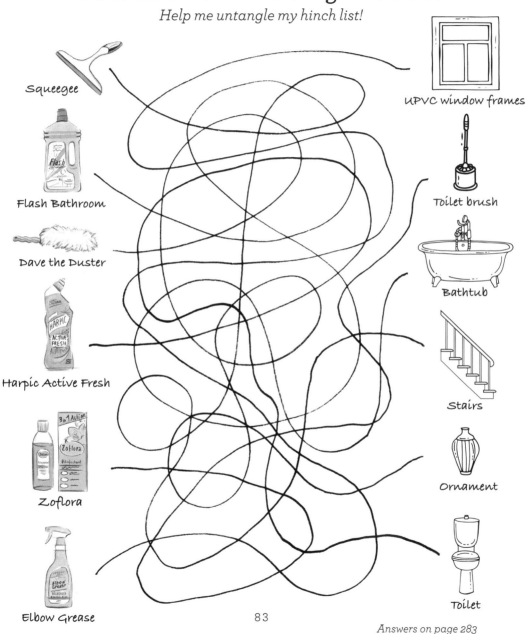

Squeegee

Flash Bathroom

Dave the Duster

Harpic Active Fresh

Zoflora

Elbow Grease

UPVC window frames

Toilet brush

Bathtub

Stairs

Ornament

Toilet

Answers on page 283

Reasons To Be Grateful Check-In

As I explained in the Count Your Blessings activity, I find that writing down a few things I'm grateful for each day helps me to remind myself just how blessed I am. Even in the very toughest of times there are always things we can be thankful for, whether it's a really good friend who is a great listener, or just having a nice cosy bed to sleep in at night.

So back on page 45 I asked you to list five things you were grateful for. I have included regular gratitude reminder pages throughout this book because I really think counting our blessings is a very important and helpful thing to do.

SO HERE WRITE DOWN FIVE MORE THINGS YOU ARE GRATEFUL FOR:

1» ....

2» ....

3» ....

4» ....

5» ....

Just remember, sometimes the simple life really is the best life.
X

Your little family

is the **BEST TEAM** you could **EVER HAVE.**

MY JOURNAL

Date: ....

Three things I'm proud I accomplished this week:

1 >> ....

....

2 >> ....

....

3 >> ....

....

What was the best day of the week and why? ....

....

....

....

What was the most challenging day of the week and why? ....

....

....

....

This week I was inspired by: ....
....

If I could relive any moment from this week, which one would it be and why?
....
....
....

Favourite quote of the week: ....
....
....

Favourite thing I hinched this week: ....
....
....

Three things to look forward to next week:

♥ ....
....

♥ ....
....

♥ ....
....

MY WEEKLY HINCH LIST

HINCH LIST *continued*

- [ ]
- [ ]
- [ ]
- [ ]
- [ ]
- [ ]
- [ ]
- [ ]
- [ ]

- [ ]
- [ ]
- [ ]
- [ ]
- [ ]
- [ ]
- [ ]
- [ ]
- [ ]

- [ ]
- [ ]
- [ ]
- [ ]
- [ ]
- [ ]
- [ ]
- [ ]
- [ ]

HINCH HAUL

- [ ]
- [ ]
- [ ]
- [ ]
- [ ]
- [ ]
- [ ]
- [ ]
- [ ]

Help Henry!

Handsomes wants his chicken stick, but it's on the other side of the maze. See how quickly you can help him find his way through, so he can get to his treat. Happy dorgeous boy!

Answer on page 284

Spot The Difference

There are 10 differences between these two
illustrations – can you spot them all?

Answers on page 284

Do Something Crafty

I love to buy things at boot sales or on boot-sale apps like Shpock or Gumtree – then transform them. It's so satisfying. I feel happy every time I look at the ottoman I painted and reupholstered. For your creative time, you might prefer to bake or sew or dance or draw. You can even doodle.

LIST THE PROJECTS YOU'D LIKE TO HINCH HERE:

☐ Project 1 » ....

How I plan to tackle it » ....

....

....

What I need to tackle it » ....

....

....

☐ Project 2 » ....

How I plan to tackle it » ....

....

....

What I need to tackle it » ....

....

....

Doodle Me!

*Carry on with this doodle, adding patterns
and shapes to fill the page.*

Your Dream Dinner Party

For this activity, I'd like you to write down who you would invite to your ultimate dinner, if you could invite anyone in the world, still with us, or not. It can be absolutely anyone! From family members, to best friends, to celebrities. Just think about the people you'd most love to sit down to dinner with, and what you'd ask them if you had the chance! I just know that Beyoncé would absolutely love my mum's roast potatoes and gravy! Just sayin'!

LIST THE PEOPLE YOU'D MOST LIKE TO INVITE AND THE QUESTION YOU'D LIKE TO ASK THEM:

1 » ....

★ ....

2 » ....

★ ....

3 » ....

★ ....

4 » ....

★ ....

5 » ....

★ ....

6 » ....

★ ....

7 » ....

★ ....

8 » ....

★ ....

MY JOURNAL

Date: ....

Three things I'm proud I accomplished this week:

1 >> ....
....
....

2 >> ....
....
....

3 >> ....
....

What was the best day of the week and why? ....
....
....
....
....

What was the most challenging day of the week and why? ....
....
....
....

This week I was inspired by: ....
....
....

If I could relive any moment from this week, which one would it be and why?
....
....
....
....

Favourite quote of the week: ....
....
....
....

Favourite thing I hinched this week: ....
....
....
....

Three things to look forward to next week:

♥ ....
....
♥ ....
....
♥ ....
....

Date: ....

MY WEEKLY HINCH LIST

HINCH LIST *continued*

- .... ☐
- .... ☐
- .... ☐
- .... ☐
- .... ☐
- .... ☐
- .... ☐
- .... ☐
- .... ☐

- .... ☐
- .... ☐
- .... ☐
- .... ☐
- .... ☐
- .... ☐
- .... ☐
- .... ☐
- .... ☐

HINCH HAUL

- .... ☐
- .... ☐
- .... ☐
- .... ☐
- .... ☐
- .... ☐
- .... ☐
- .... ☐
- .... ☐

- .... ☐
- .... ☐
- .... ☐
- .... ☐
- .... ☐
- .... ☐
- .... ☐
- .... ☐
- .... ☐

Don't forget to share your hinch lists!

#mrshinchtheactivityjournal

Change The Way
You Think About Yourself

If someone was to ask me if I thought there were any bits of myself that needed hinching, I'd be able to give them a much longer checklist than if they asked me to name positive things about myself. For some reason, it's too easy for us to focus on what we believe are the negative bits about ourselves instead of celebrating all of our amazing qualities. But something as simple as wording things in a different way can make such a big difference to how we see ourselves. For example, you all know that I spend a lot of time worrying, which could be seen as a weakness. But if you think about it, I worry as much as I do because of how much I care. I also over-think things a lot. But rather than seeing myself as an over-thinker, I try to see myself as someone who is good at thinking things through.

Have a go at rewording the things you think you need to work on below. If you're struggling, why don't you try working on this activity with a friend so you can both help each other!

Puppy Henry

*Colour in this picture of my dorgeous
boy when he was a baby. Once
complete, don't forget to share and*
#mrshinchtheactivityjournal

And Breathe…

As I'm still learning, it's important to stop and breathe once in a while. Nothing else, just breathe and be mindful of the moment you're in. I know breathing sounds easy, but when things get on top of us it's hard not to stress and panic. So here are a couple of activities to help you – and me – learn to relax properly and pay attention to our breathing. It's important that you feel comfortable, so these are just suggestions – you might find a way that works better for you.

MINDFUL BREATHING EXERCISE

★ Sit comfortably, resting your hands gently on your lap, and straighten your upper body.

★ Let the soles of your feet ground themselves on the floor.

★ Relax your shoulders and lower your chin slightly.

★ Allow your face to relax, releasing any tension around your jaw and mouth and between your eyes.

★ Slowly close your eyes or lower your gaze.

★ Relax and bring your attention to your breath.

Then, once you are comfortable, you can begin a breathing cycle:

★ Breathe in slowly for 4 counts.

★ Pause for 2 counts.

★ Breathe out slowly for 4 counts. Notice the stillness during the pause.

★ Repeat.

Counting the breath is an amazing way to slow down our breathing and quieten the mind. You could try thinking of the word 'Let' as you inhale and 'Go' as you exhale.

As you breathe, you might notice your mind wandering and your thoughts coming and going like crazy. Instead of trying to stop them, just bring your attention back to your breathing. When you are ready, slowly open your eyes or lift your gaze, and observe how your mind and body feel as you return your attention to the room. Then sit back and chill.

DISSOLVE A THOUGHT

Sometimes our minds can get stuck on the same worrying or upsetting thought. I know mine does, all the time. When things are going really well, I always think something has to go wrong; it's too good to be true. Rather than enjoying the good, I worry. This little exercise can really help.

1 » Breathe in deeply through your nose. Count 1–2–3–4.

2 » Breathe out fully through your mouth. Count 1–2–3–4.

3 » Picture each thought you have as a cloud above your head.

4 » As you breathe in (1–2–3–4), notice this cloud.

5 » As you breathe out (1–2–3–4), let the cloud dissolve.

6 » Repeat with a new thought.

DIARY DELIGHT

MON

*Let's be honest... most of the time we only think to do the stuff
that makes us feel better when we are already stressed or tired.
I'd like to encourage us to take more time for ourselves; more
me-time. Hinching makes me feel better, but so does seeing my
friends and having a laugh, doing a word search, going for a walk,
relaxing with Jamie and some snacks on the sofa, watching a
programme on the telly... Yours might be baking or gardening,
sewing or crafts. So please use these boxes to plan doing at least
one thing a day that's just for you – every day of the week. Even
if it's for only five minutes at a time. Don't forget to update your
personal calendar to make sure you stick to your plans!*

TUES

WED

THURS

FRI

SAT

SUN

TRAVEL AT YOUR OWN PACE
THERE'LL BE TIME ENOUGH
TO LEARN ALL YOU NEED TO KNOW
AND GO AS FAR AS
YOU'RE MEANT TO GO
PAULA FINN

MY JOURNAL

Date: ....

Three things I'm proud I accomplished this week:

1 >> ....
....
....

2 >> ....
....
....

3 >> ....
....
....

What was the best day of the week and why? ....
....
....
....
....

What was the most challenging day of the week and why? ....
....
....
....
....

This week I was inspired by: ....

....

If I could relive any moment from this week, which one would it be and why?

....

....

....

Favourite quote of the week: ....

....

....

Favourite thing I hinched this week: ....

....

....

Three things to look forward to next week:

♥ ....

♥ ....

♥ ....

Date: ....

MY WEEKLY HINCH LIST

HINCH LIST *continued*

- [ ]
- [ ]
- [ ]
- [ ]
- [ ]
- [ ]
- [ ]
- [ ]

- [ ]
- [ ]
- [ ]
- [ ]
- [ ]
- [ ]
- [ ]
- [ ]

- [ ]
- [ ]
- [ ]
- [ ]
- [ ]
- [ ]
- [ ]
- [ ]

HINCH HAUL

- [ ]
- [ ]
- [ ]
- [ ]
- [ ]
- [ ]
- [ ]
- [ ]

Hinch Your Sudoku

Fill in the missing squares!

HINCH HINT: Fill the grid with the four hinching objects so that each object is only used once in each row, column and 2×2 block.

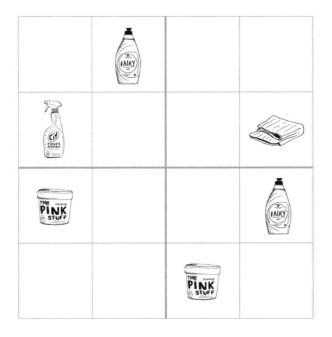

Answers on page 284

Hinching For The Mind

I started hinching because it makes me feel calmer. I know a lot of you feel exactly the same because you've told me. When I get random anxious thoughts, dusting with Dave or mopping with Vera do the trick!

SIGNS I NEED TO HINCH:

★ My thoughts start to run away with me

★ I struggle to concentrate

★ I can't sit still

MY TOP 3 CALMING HINCHES:

There's nothing like looking at a shiny mirror or tiles, or smelling the freshly hinched sofa! These are the hinches that work best for me.

1 » Shining the kitchen sink

2 » Hinching the bathroom (there's nothing like a freshly pined loo and the smell of Flash Bathroom . . .)

3 » Squeegeeing the stairs

WHICH HINCHING JOBS LEAVE YOU FEELING THE MOST CALM? FILL IN YOUR TOP 5:

1 » ....

2 » ....

3 » ....

4 » ....

5 » ....

So the next time you're feeling anxious or worried, come back to this list and it might help.

A Letter To Your 14-Year-Old Self

Some of you may already know that I didn't have the best time at school. Looking back, it taught me not only a lot about myself, but also a lot about how to deal with people. If you had a difficult time when you were little, as a child or a teenager, I thought it would be helpful for us to show ourselves what we've learnt by writing a letter to our younger selves. I also know that I have a lot of younger Hinchers who may find it comforting to know that life is worth holding on tight for, because it really does get so much better – more so than you can ever imagine.

I've left some space for you to write your own letter over the page. This is what I'd write . . .

Dear Miss Sophie Barker,

Right now, you feel like the loneliest girl in the world. But I want you to know that there are a lot of people that feel exactly the same way you do, and you aren't alone. I promise you. What people behave like on the outside is often nothing like how they feel on the inside. And when people are horrible to others, it's usually because they are going through something themselves, and they feel hurt, or scared, or sad. At the moment, you feel as if your life is going to be like this forever. You feel trapped in this place, like you're never going to escape. But I'm here to tell you that you are going to be so happy one day. Happier than you could ever imagine.

Very soon, you're going to meet a group of girls, and they're going to change your life. They're going to make you laugh harder than you've ever laughed before, and they're going to look after you, and have your back. And that's just the start. You're going to meet the man of your dreams, Jamie, and he is going to make you feel more loved than you ever even knew was possible, and keep you so safe. You'll both own your dream home one day, with the world's most perfect fur baby, which you'll call Handsomes Henry Dorgeous Mans. And, as if all of that wasn't incredible enough, you're going to find out the most amazing surprise: that all your dreams have come true, and you're going to have a perfect little baby boy, who you'll call Ronnie.

And for the girl who started off at school without any friends, you'll be lucky enough to be a part of this amazing community of incredibly supportive Hinchers who you will get to speak to every day. They will literally change your life.

So please keep going, kidda. It'll all be worth it in the end, I promise. Everything will work out.

Lots of love,
Mrs Sophie Hinchliffe
aka Mrs Hinch
xxx

Dear

Favourite Books

Write the titles of your favourite books on the spines on the bookshelf below. Then write who your favourite character is and why!

FAVOURITE CHARACTER AND WHY

1 » ....

2 » ....

3 » ....

4 » ....

5 » ....

6 » ....

7 » ....

The Category Challenge

Fill in the blanks with words that begin with the letter

N

Shop name ....

Author ....

Celebrity ....

Cleaning product ....

Flower ....

Car model ....

Dog breed ....

Country ....

Item of clothing ....

Fruit ....

Insect ....

Something cold ....

Body part ....

Animal ....

Household item ....

Hobby ....

Spice or herb ....

Restaurant ....

Occupation ....

Something that
makes you smile ....

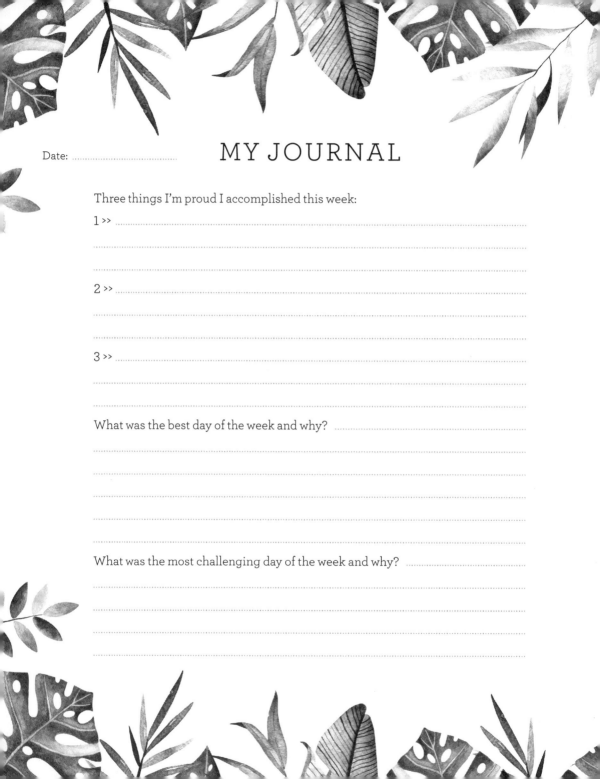

Date: ....

MY JOURNAL

Three things I'm proud I accomplished this week:

1 >> ....

....

....

2 >> ....

....

....

3 >> ....

....

....

What was the best day of the week and why? ....

....

....

....

....

What was the most challenging day of the week and why? ....

....

....

....

This week I was inspired by: ....
....

If I could relive any moment from this week, which one would it be and why?
....
....
....
....

Favourite quote of the week: ....
....
....

Favourite thing I hinched this week: ....
....
....

Three things to look forward to next week:
♥ ....
....
♥ ....
....
♥ ....
....

MY WEEKLY HINCH LIST

HINCH LIST *continued*

- [ ] ....
- [ ] ....
- [ ] ....
- [ ] ....
- [ ] ....
- [ ] ....
- [ ] ....
- [ ] ....
- [ ] ....

- [ ] ....
- [ ] ....
- [ ] ....
- [ ] ....
- [ ] ....
- [ ] ....
- [ ] ....
- [ ] ....
- [ ] ....

HINCH HAUL

- [ ] ....
- [ ] ....
- [ ] ....
- [ ] ....
- [ ] ....
- [ ] ....
- [ ] ....
- [ ] ....
- [ ] ....

- [ ] ....
- [ ] ....
- [ ] ....
- [ ] ....
- [ ] ....
- [ ] ....
- [ ] ....
- [ ] ....
- [ ] ....

I'd love to see your hinch lists!

#mrshinchtheactivityjournal

The Little Things In Life

You don't have to go on holiday to a beautiful beach to be truly happy. You know I'm a big believer in being at home and the joys of normal, everyday life. If you can find joy in the small things, it really will make your days feel more positive and happy.

Get up 20 minutes earlier and have a cup of tea looking out of the window.

Declutter one of your drawers.

Rearrange the furniture in one room.

Do your hair and make-up nicely.

Stroke a fur baby.

Invite a friend over for a cup of tea.

Go for a walk – somewhere green if you can.

Reorganise a shelf or your shoe cupboard.

Don't just tick off your hinch list – enjoy the actual cleaning too.

Plant some seeds for herbs on your windowsill or in pots in your garden.

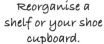

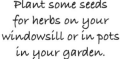

Take a duvet day: read a book or watch a movie tucked up in bed or on the sofa.

LIST YOUR FAVOURITE SOCIAL MEDIA ACCOUNTS HERE:

Account name: ....

Why it makes me feel inspired and happy: ....

....

....

Account name: ....

Why it makes me feel inspired and happy: ....

....

....

Account name: ....

Why it makes me feel inspired and happy: ....

....

....

Account name: ....

Why it makes me feel inspired and happy: ....

....

....

Account name: ....

Why it makes me feel inspired and happy: ....

....

....

Colour me

STAYING IN
VS
GOING OUT
THIS *or* THAT
Underline your fave from each pair!

Slippers  Heels

Make-up  Face mask

Cuppa  Cocktails

Cosy  Lit

Naps  Late nights

Cinema  Netflix

Karaoke  Rave

Loungewear  Dress

Dance floor  Sofa

Takeaway  Restaurant

I'd love to see your choices on Instagram, Hinchers! Don't
forget to share and **#mrshinchtheactivityjournal**, and why
not upload a blank copy so your friends can join in too!

My Hinching Soundtrack!

These are some of my favourite songs to hinch to.

ACROSS

5. 'U Got It Bad' is by ....

6. 'Started From the Bottom' is by ....

8. The Brandy and Monica anthem is ....

9. A Beyoncé classic

10. .... sings another fave: 'Can You Feel the Love Tonight'

DOWN

1. You can Never have Too Much Luther ....

2. Sharon's song is 'Baby ....'

3. Gotta have a bit of Destiny's Child. They sang 'I'm a ....'

4. There's only one ...., possibly the Greatest Love of All

7. Everyone knows this is my Cliff the Cif song: .... by Aretha Franklin

Answers on page 285

Positive Affirmations

I'll be honest … the first time I heard about positive affirmations I thought they were, well, odd. The idea of sitting on the edge of my bed on a morning before I start my day and repeating positive statements to myself out loud just absolutely did not seem like a bit of me. What on earth would Jamie even think if he caught me doing it?! But trust me, Hinchers, I've actually found them really helpful.

An affirmation is a positive phrase that you repeat to yourself regularly – it doesn't have to be out loud – to help get rid of negative thoughts, to help you to feel more in control and to set you up with a positive mindset for the day. You can say your positive affirmations whenever you like. I like to do mine before I get going on a morning. I won't lie: it feels ridiculous the first couple of times you do it, but then you don't even notice! The more you practise, the easier and more natural it will become.

I change mine up depending on what I'm feeling at the time, but examples of some of the ones I use are: 'I am going to have a good day today and will not be controlled by my anxiety' and 'I accept and love myself for who I am.' Can you think of any affirmations you'd like to say to yourself each morning to start your day in the most positive way? Write them down in the positivity jar on the opposite page.

FUR BABY FRIENDLY RECIPE

3 cups flour
½ cup oats
1 tsp baking powder
¼ cup grated carrots
¼ cup water
1 cup peanut butter

1. Preheat oven to 180°C/gas mark 4.

2. Mix the ingredients, roll out, and cut out with a bone-shaped biscuit cutter.

3. Bake for 10 minutes. Then flip the biscuits over and bake until golden brown (usually about 10 more minutes).

4. Cool and serve.

I thought it would be a lot of fun to make our handsomes some yummy treats! Henry absolutely loves these biscuits! Why don't you have a go at making them for the special fur puppy in your life and let me know if they love them just as much! I've left some more space here for you to write down any fur baby friendly recipes you love to use. Don't forget to tag me, Hinchers! I would love to have a go at making yours too!

Have **FAITH** in yourself. If you do, you will be amazed at what you can **ACCOMPLISH.**

T.L. Nash

MY JOURNAL

Date: ....

Three things I'm proud I accomplished this week:

1 >> ....
....
....

2 >> ....
....
....

3 >> ....
....
....

What was the best day of the week and why? ....
....
....
....
....

What was the most challenging day of the week and why? ....
....
....
....
....

This week I was inspired by: ....

....

If I could relive any moment from this week, which one would it be and why?

....

....

....

....

Favourite quote of the week: ....

....

....

....

Favourite thing I hinched this week: ....

....

....

....

Three things to look forward to next week:

♥ ....

....

♥ ....

....

♥ ....

....

MY WEEKLY HINCH LIST

HINCH LIST *continued*

☐ _____

☐ _____

☐ _____

☐ _____

☐ _____

☐ _____

☐ _____

☐ _____

☐ _____

HINCH HAUL

Life Lessons

We often learn our biggest lessons in life from the people closest to us. Whether it's one of our best friends, or a parent, or maybe even a teacher from school – the people we spend the most time with tend to have the biggest impact on our lives.

It's all too easy for us to forget the important lessons that have been passed on to us from the influential people in our lives. If I think about who I've learnt the most from, I always come back to my mum, who has been there for me through thick and thin. One of the things my mum is always telling me is that you can only ever try your best. And if that isn't good enough for some people, then that's their problem. So one of my lessons would be:

Teacher: *My mum*

Lesson: *You can only try your best*

How this has helped me in life: *It has taught me my best is good enough*

Have a think about all the most impactful people in your life and write their names and the lessons they have taught you below.

Teacher:

Lesson:

How this has helped me in life:

Teacher:

Lesson:

How this has helped me in life:

Teacher:

Lesson:

How this has helped me in life:

Magical Terrace

Colour this relaxing outdoor space.
Don't forget to share and
#mrshinchtheactivityjournal

The Mrs Hinch Photo Challenge

As you all know, Instagram is one of my favourite things. It has helped me so much, in so many ways, and it's where I've met and managed to stay connected to all of you! I've always loved taking photos. I think a picture can tell a story so much better than any words ever could.

I know I say it so much, but being grateful for what you have and feeling happy about it is really important to me. I genuinely think it can make a huge difference to how you feel about your life. It's so easy to get caught up in the little things going wrong and forget to stop for a moment and appreciate all of those amazing things that are going right.

I've always loved these photo challenges on Instagram. So I thought we could all do one together, Mrs Hinch style, to remind us just how truly amazing our lives are just as they are.

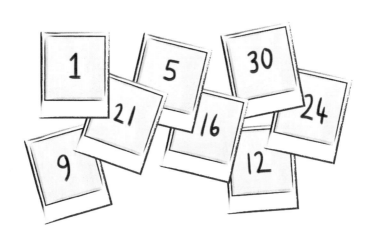

FOR THE NEXT 30 DAYS I WANT YOU TO TAKE A PHOTO THAT MAKES YOU FEEL REALLY HAPPY, AND COVER EACH OF THE FOLLOWING:

☐ Family

☐ Home

☐ Love

☐ Happiness

☐ Creativity

☐ Relaxing

☐ Organise

☐ Laughter

☐ Cleaning

☐ Gratitude

☐ Calm

☐ Beauty

☐ Nature

☐ Learning

☐ Me-time

☐ Home improvements

☐ Colour

☐ Inspired

☐ Narnia

☐ Sunshine

☐ Cosy

☐ Bargain

☐ Flowers

☐ Cosy corner

☐ Upcycle

☐ Scent

☐ Fave find

☐ Before and after

☐ Hinched

☐ Throwback

Please share your photos with **#mrshinchphotochallenge**

Ava May Wax Melt Scent Word Search

It's no secret these are my fave wax melts. Can you spot some of the popular scents?

```
R K Q L M H X N B A T R Q I O L U X M E A E Y D M
U E Q B G G A Y X C L T W J L T A U U X N R P O O
W C D O A I N Y B L M I J N W A P Q I N D I H N U
F U F W P U G I F O K S E H E D C U P Y M A D T N
L W P M O Z Q I N P G P M N C C H X O K A N L S T
M R Y M H P Y Q V E Z A C L I F H V K H N O E T A
Y L J Y W R Y K Q V K Y G M K N D H R P D I S O I
O K L M O Z H B K A M A O S D I V O A Y A L I P N
P P D M R K P Q A U V P W E V Y R A D A R L N M A
K E I E S X H A D B F C Q A Q C N S S N I I A E I
T W I L I G H T G A R D E N G E X O R I N M D N R
S J M I T N G H H S U Y X H D N U E L C O K N O L
K W F S S R S W P U D E T R K N I T Q Y F N A W E
J D R S A O R R K I L D A I Q U T R D A P N A K Q
P I W E Q L I A H H X G L B L C O R P H G A L Y V
V S Q T J N P C X K Y F I S R I V A P S E O L B Z
U U D S G X R R Y R C R N L D O U L H R N T I B F
S R X T V O L B T P V U E A G K J Q O F X A N Z J
S Z I F K R I N V V S T N D D I D D N U C L A V U
F M D C B S U D P C J A F Y V F A X V A C O V S E
E Y A O G O E H N K S W R M A X S D P Q R G K K U
J L T R C F R G C I I N E R X A T C K U B T G S D
B L I S A B E M I L L I S H U Q S A V A G E X T L
S E Y C H E L L E S R Z H N K B J F Y X R W L J Q
E Q V C I N I R A D N A M D N A L I S A B E M I L
```

- ☐ Alien Invasion
- ☐ Adore
- ☐ Baby Powder
- ☐ Black Orchid
- ☐ Dark Opium
- ☐ Don't Stop Me Now
- ☐ Lady
- ☐ Lime Basil and Mandarin
- ☐ Millionaire
- ☐ Olympian
- ☐ Savage
- ☐ Seychelles
- ☐ Spring Awakening
- ☐ Tranquility
- ☐ Vanilla and Anise
- ☐ Linen Fresh
- ☐ Twilight Garden
- ☐ Springtime
- ☐ Country Garden
- ☐ Mountain Air

Answers on page 285

Bucket List

I know I've already asked you to think about your goals,
but your bucket list is something different.

Rather than things you'd like to achieve, your bucket list should
be a list of things you'd like to experience in your life, no matter
how big or how small! Now, you know how much I love my normal,
'boring' life. I think it's the absolute best! But there are still things
I'd love to do, and places I'd love to see. I think it's sometimes
too easy for us to get stuck in a rut, but life is precious and time
is short, so I'd like you to sit and have a think about all those
things you'd love do in your life, and list them here. And don't
just list them, Hinchers; think about how you can start making
them happen!

1 » ....

2 » ....

3 » ....

4 » ....

5 » ....

6 » ....

7 » ....

8 » ....

9 » ....

10 » ....

MY JOURNAL

Date: ....

Three things I'm proud I accomplished this week:

1 >> ....

....

....

2 >> ....

....

....

3 >> ....

....

What was the best day of the week and why? ....

....

....

....

....

What was the most challenging day of the week and why? ....

....

....

....

This week I was inspired by: ....
....

If I could relive any moment from this week, which one would it be and why?
....
....
....
....

Favourite quote of the week: ....
....
....

Favourite thing I hinched this week: ....
....
....

Three things to look forward to next week:

♥ ....
....

♥ ....
....

♥ ....
....

Date: ....

MY WEEKLY HINCH LIST

HINCH LIST *continued*

	☐		☐
	☐		☐
	☐		☐
	☐		☐
	☐		☐
	☐		☐
	☐		☐
	☐		☐
	☐		☐

HINCH HAUL

	☐		☐
	☐		☐
	☐		☐
	☐		☐
	☐		☐
	☐		☐
	☐		☐
	☐		☐
	☐		☐

Don't forget to share your hinch lists!

#mrshinchtheactivityjournal

The Category Challenge

Fill in the blanks with words that begin with the letter

C

Shop name ....

Author ....

Celebrity ....

Cleaning product ....

Flower ....

Car model ....

Dog breed ....

Country ....

Item of clothing ....

Fruit ....

Insect ....

Something cold ....

Body part ....

Animal ....

Household item ....

Hobby ....

Spice or herb ....

Restaurant ....

Occupation ....

Something that
makes you smile ....

Goal 1 Review

Please go back to page 19 and check your first goal.

My goal» ....

What things have you already done to progress your goal?

1» ....

2» ....

3» ....

What have been your biggest obstacles so far?

1» ....

2» ....

3» ....

List some things that you still need to do to achieve your goal:

1» ....

2» ....

3» ....

Goal 2 Review

Please go back to page 20 and check your second goal.

My goal » ....

What things have you already done to progress your goal?

1 » ....

2 » ....

3 » ....

What have been your biggest obstacles so far?

1 » ....

2 » ....

3 » ....

List some things that you still need to do to achieve your goal:

1 » ....

2 » ....

3 » ....

Goal Check-In

Goal 3 Review

Please go back to page 21 and check your third goal.

My goal»

What things have you already done to progress your goal?

1»

2»

3»

What have been your biggest obstacles so far?

1»

2»

3»

List some things that you still need to do to achieve your goal:

1»

2»

3»

DOT-TO-DOT

Don't forget to colour me in afterwards!

Spread A Little Happiness

One of the things I like to do every day is make someone smile. That's why I try to make my Instagram stories as happy and as motivating as possible. If I can make you Hinchers smile even just once a day, then that's good enough for me! And hopefully someone will return the favour to you. I think we should be spreading kindness around like confetti. I always say it costs nothing to be nice, so here are some things you could do today to put a smile on someone else's face. And just think of how amazing it feels to make someone else feel good. Fill in the bubbles with more ideas of things you've done to spread a little happiness.

Compliment someone.

When you talk to the next person who serves you in a cafe or shop, smile and look them in the eye.

Buy a hot drink for the person behind you in the queue.

Tell a joke.

Offer a lift to someone you know who hasn't got a car.

Help someone who's struggling with bags or a buggy.

Think of a friend who's busy and ask if there's anything they'd like you to hinch for them.

Put a nice comment on someone's Facebook wall or Instagram.

Let someone else have a seat on the bus.

Hold the door open for the person behind you.

Bake a cake for the office.

Hello!

Text someone and just simply ask how they are.

Let another car in front of you.

Call a friend and tell them you love them.

At the supermarket, donate to a food bank.

Tell someone their baby/child/dog is beautiful.

Bedtime Baskets

As you might already know from my first book and from watching my stories, Hinchers, there are some things I like to do before I go to bed. I have a bedtime hinch list which includes: karate chopping my cushions, Febreze-ing the sofa, Zoflora-ing the kitchen worktops, and putting the cloth babies to bed. I'm not always the best at getting off to sleep (you will have seen me use pillow sleep spray to help), and because of this I keep a bedtime basket next to my bed with all the things I need to help me have a good night's rest. Below is what's in my bedtime basket. Have a go at writing a list for your own! Better still, create one in real life and send me a picture. I'd love it if we could all have a go at doing them together. After all, how amazing does a decent night's sleep feel! And it sets us all up nicely for a new day of hinching!

MY BEDTIME BASKET:

★ Eye mask

★ Ear plugs

★ Phone charger

★ Pillow spray

★ Lip balm

★ A mini notepad and pen

★ Headphones

YOUR BEDTIME BASKET:

★ ....

★ ....

★ ....

★ ....

★ ....

★ ....

★ ....

★ ....

★ ....

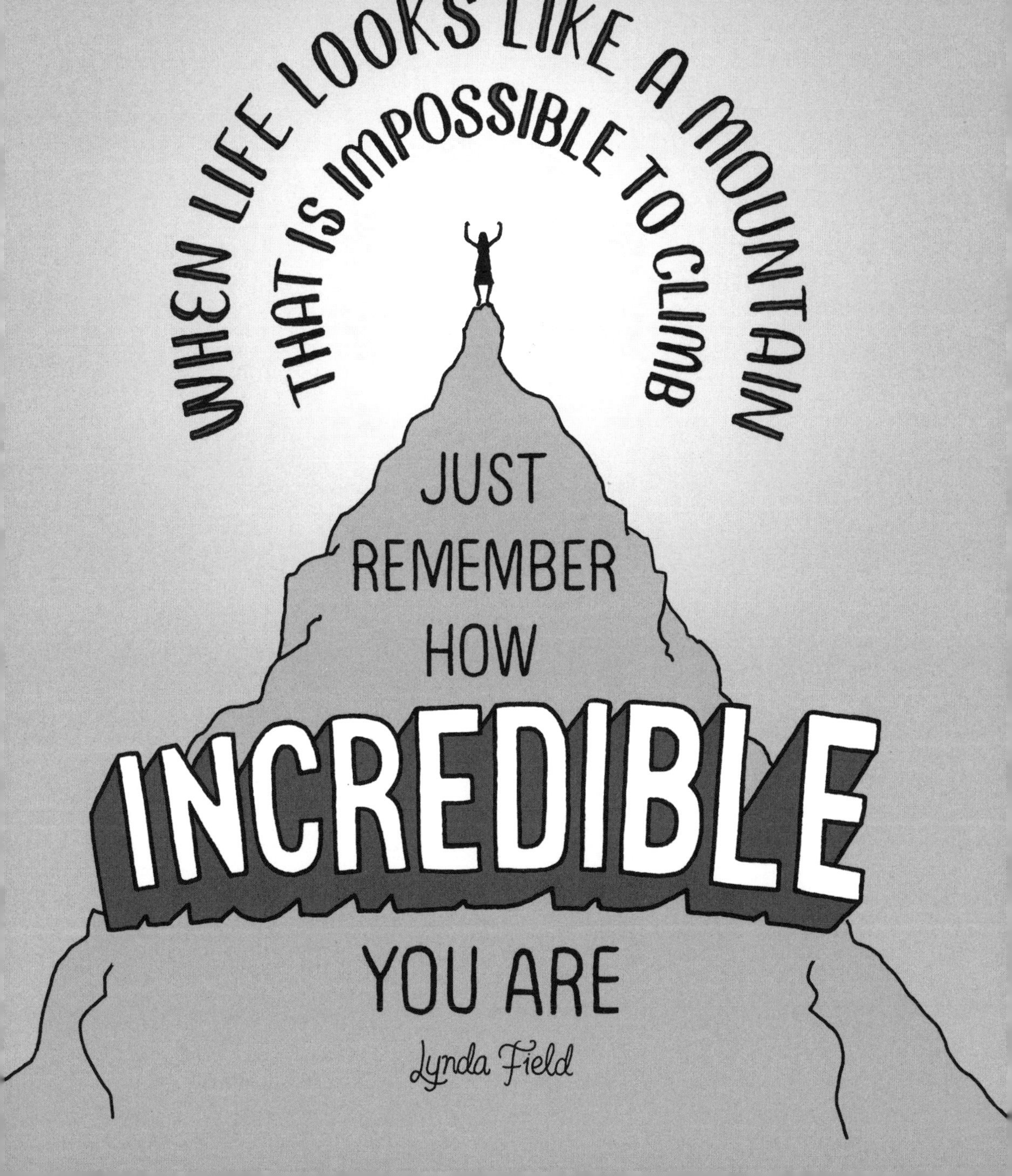

WHEN LIFE LOOKS LIKE A MOUNTAIN THAT IS IMPOSSIBLE TO CLIMB

JUST REMEMBER HOW

INCREDIBLE

YOU ARE

Lynda Field

MY JOURNAL

Date: ....

Three things I'm proud I accomplished this week:

1 >> ....
....
....

2 >> ....
....
....

3 >> ....
....

What was the best day of the week and why? ....
....
....
....
....

What was the most challenging day of the week and why? ....
....
....
....
....

This week I was inspired by: ....
....
....

If I could relive any moment from this week, which one would it be and why?
....
....
....
....

Favourite quote of the week: ....
....
....

Favourite thing I hinched this week: ....
....
....

Three things to look forward to next week:
♥ ....
....
♥ ....
....
♥ ....
....

Date: ....

MY WEEKLY HINCH LIST

HINCH LIST *continued*

☐
☐
☐
☐
☐
☐
☐
☐

☐
☐
☐
☐
☐
☐
☐
☐

HINCH HAUL

☐
☐
☐
☐
☐
☐
☐
☐
☐

☐
☐
☐
☐
☐
☐
☐
☐
☐

Colour In The Cloth Family

*Colour in my little cloth fam with the correct colours
and match the name to the family member.*

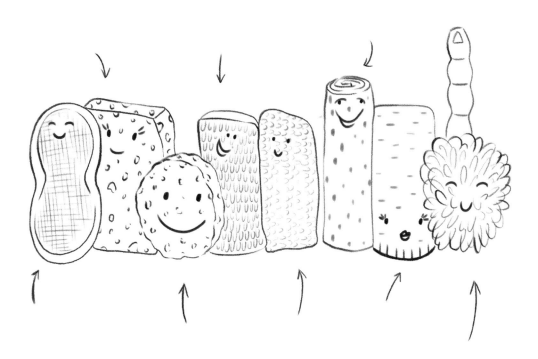

Minkeh   Brian   Dave

Pinkeh   Kermit   Scrub Daddy

Buddy   Clarence

Answers on page 286

The Soulmates Quiz

Find out just how well you know your other half!

Mr Hinch and I had such a laugh playing this game. Bless him, he absolutely smashed it! Choose, say, 10 questions from any of the below. You can add some of your own personal ones too! Let your partner or bestie answer the questions on a piece of paper first, then you do the same. This quiz works brilliantly for Mr and Mr, and for Mrs and Mrs too, and for best mates, of course.

Once you've both answered, compare your answers. Ideally, they should be the same. But even when they aren't, it can be a lot of fun to disagree!

1 » Who is their celebrity crush?

2 » What is their star sign?

3 » What do they most like about you?

4 » What would they be saddest to give up for a week?

5 » What's their favourite famous landmark?

6 » What are the three things they'd save in a fire?

7 » Which one of you is tidier?

8 » What's the one phrase or word they say the most?

9 » What's their favourite hinching product?

10 » What's the best gift you've ever given them?

11 » Do they prefer a bath or a shower?

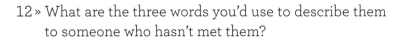

12 » What are the three words you'd use to describe them to someone who hasn't met them?

13 » How do they like their tea/coffee?

14 » What's their favourite kind of cake?

15 » What was the last thing that made them cry?

16 » What was the first thing that attracted you to them?

17 » What's their favourite flavour of crisps?

18 » What's their favourite hinching task?

19 » What celebrity do they think they look most like?

20 » What was the first present they ever gave you?

21 » What's their favourite shop?

22 » Where would be their dream destination to visit?

23 » What's their favourite movie?

24 » Which one of you does the most hinching?

25 » What's their guiltiest pleasure?

26 » What's their messiest habit?

27 » Would they rather spend a night in with you or out with their mates?

28 » Are they a cat person or a dog person?

Doodle Me!

*Carry on with this doodle, adding patterns
and shapes to fill the page.*

Spot The Difference

*There are 5 differences between these two illustrations –
can you spot them all?*

Answers on page 286

Your Perfect Day

I'd love to know what your best day ever would look like, Hinchers!
What would it involve? What would you be doing? Who would you
be with? Here are my answers to get you started...

What day of the week would it be? *Sunday!*

Where would you wake up? *At home with my boys*

What would you feel like? *Relaxed, organised and healthy*

Would it be a special day – your birthday, for example? Or Christmas? *Just a normal 'boring' day. They're the best!*

Would you go to work? *I would hinch! Hinch until I'm happy!*

What time would you wake up? *I like an early rise! Between 7:00 and 8:00 is perf!*

What kind of hinching would you do and when? *I would have a little look in each room, write out my hinch list and off I'd go!*

Who would you spend it with? *Family and friends*

What would you have for breakfast? *I won't lie . . . . I do love a fry-up!*

What would you do in the morning? *Walk Henry, have breakfast, and have a chat with Jamie. Probably sounds silly but I don't think people sit down to have a nice chat enough any more. They're always on their phones! I don't like to sit on my phone too much in the mornings.*

What would you have for lunch? *My mum's Sunday roast! (See p.182 for the recipe!)*

How would you spend your afternoon? *Hinching!*

What would you do in the evening? *Snuggle up on the sofa with my fleece blanket and my boys, and watch TV!*

How would you feel at the end of this day? *Grateful*

NOW WRITE OUT YOUR PERFECT DAY:

What day of the week would it be? ....

Where would you wake up? ....

What would you feel like? ....

Would it be a special day – your birthday, for example? Or Christmas?

....

Would you go to work? ....

What time would you wake up? ....

What kind of hinching would you do and when? ....

Who would you spend it with? ....

What would you have for breakfast? ....

What would you do in the morning? ....

What would you have for lunch? ....

How would you spend your afternoon? ....

What would you do in the evening? ....

How would you feel at the end of this day? ....

....

....

MY JOURNAL

Date: ....

Three things I'm proud I accomplished this week:

1 >> ....
....
....

2 >> ....
....
....

3 >> ....
....
....

What was the best day of the week and why? ....
....
....
....
....

What was the most challenging day of the week and why? ....
....
....
....

This week I was inspired by: ....
....

If I could relive any moment from this week, which one would it be and why?
....
....
....

Favourite quote of the week: ....
....
....

Favourite thing I hinched this week: ....
....
....

Three things to look forward to next week:
♥ ....
♥ ....
♥ ....

Date: ....

MY WEEKLY HINCH LIST

HINCH LIST *continued*

- [ ] ....
- [ ] ....
- [ ] ....
- [ ] ....
- [ ] ....
- [ ] ....
- [ ] ....
- [ ] ....
- [ ] ....

- [ ] ....
- [ ] ....
- [ ] ....
- [ ] ....
- [ ] ....
- [ ] ....
- [ ] ....
- [ ] ....
- [ ] ....

HINCH HAUL

- [ ] ....
- [ ] ....
- [ ] ....
- [ ] ....
- [ ] ....
- [ ] ....
- [ ] ....
- [ ] ....
- [ ] ....

- [ ] ....
- [ ] ....
- [ ] ....
- [ ] ....
- [ ] ....
- [ ] ....
- [ ] ....
- [ ] ....
- [ ] ....

I'd love to see your hinch lists!

#mrshinchtheactivityjournal

A Few Of My Favourite Things

ACROSS

2. Born on 20 June 2019, my little angel, ...

4. You know how I love my .... Hour

6. One of the best days of my life was my ....

8. I spent my honeymoon in the ....

9. Always and forever – my love,
Mr .... Hinch

10. A big focus for my home recently
has been my ....

DOWN

1. My alter ego is called ....

3. My favourite way to clean a room
is to do a ....

5. My version of a to-do list ....

7. My beloved ....,
Henry Hinch ♡

8. My favourite type of cleaning cloth
is my ....

Answers on page 286

MY LOVELY MUM'S ROAST

*Everyone knows
I like nothing better
than my lovely mum's
Sunday roast!*

Paxo stuffing
1 large whole chicken
Plain flour
Semi-skimmed milk
2 eggs
Maris Piper potatoes
Salt
Cooking oil
Cauliflower
Schwartz cheese sauce
    sachet
Grated cheese
Choice of veg
    (we have broccoli,
    carrots, Brussels)
Bisto gravy granules
2 OXO cubes
Worcester sauce

*The good thing
about cooking is
that everyone
cooks so
differently.
Tag me your
version of a
roast dinner!*

1. Preheat the oven to 170°C/gas mark 3.

2. Stuff the chicken, then place on an ovenproof dish and follow cooking guidelines (each chicken size is a different cooking time).

3. Mix 1 mug of plain flour, 1 mug of semi-skimmed milk and 2 eggs and place in the fridge to sit until the Yorkshires need to go in the oven.

4. Time to prepare the roast potatoes. Wash and peel them, cut them into even sizes, place in boiling water and add a pinch of salt.

5. Place your cooking oil into a baking tray and place in the oven until hot.

6. Add the parboiled potatoes to the oil and put in the oven (top shelf) for 45 minutes turning them once in between.

7. Time to prepare the cauliflower cheese! Parboil the cauliflower and mix up your cheese sauce sachet.

8. Put the cheese sauce over the cauliflower, sprinkle with grated cheese and put to one side for now.

9. Wash and prepare your remaining veg, then lightly simmer until the veg is cooked to how you like it! (We like ours really soft.)

10. Put a teaspoon of oil into each pudding tin and place into the oven until piping hot. Then, take your Yorkshire pudding mix from the fridge, give it a good stir, and evenly pour the mix into each pudding tin.

11. Place in the oven (middle shelf) and leave to rise until golden.

12. Place your cauliflower cheese into the oven and leave until cheese has baked.

13. Gravy time! Using the stock from your cooked veg, mix this with your desired chicken gravy granules (Mum uses reduced salt Bisto granules, two OXO cubes and a small dash of Worcester sauce).

14. Dish up once it's all cooked and you're done!

Generosity Challenge

One of the things that I like most about myself is my determination to help others. I think when we talk about being generous, a lot of people think we mean with our funds. But there are so many other ways to be generous; for example, with our time, by sharing a little bit of ourselves in the hope it will improve someone else's day. Little gestures can go such a long way! Take the time to compliment someone on their clothes, or give them a quick smile. Say thank you to someone when they've gone out of their way to help you. Write someone a little note to cheer them up, or just to let them know that you're thinking about them. All of these are lovely things to do, and I love it when I'm on the receiving end. It makes me feel all warm and fuzzy! So it's a win-win situation! It feels amazing to give, and amazing to receive!

USE THIS SPACE TO WRITE DOWN 5 IDEAS OF HOW YOU COULD SHARE YOUR TIME WITH OTHERS:

1»

2»

3»

4»

5»

Where's Sophie?

Hinchers, you won't believe it but I've only gone and got myself lost in the cleaning aisle! Help a girl out and find me! Challenge: colour in all the products differently!

Answer on page 286

Favourite Movies

List your favourite movies and give them a star rating.
What's your favourite scene and why?

Favourite film: ....

Favourite scene: ....

Why: ....

☆☆☆☆☆

Favourite film: ....

Favourite scene: ....

Why: ....

☆☆☆☆☆

Favourite film: ....

Favourite scene: ....

Why: ....

☆☆☆☆☆

Favourite film: ....

Favourite scene: ....

Why: ....

☆☆☆☆☆

Favourite film: ....

Favourite scene: ....

Why: ....

☆☆☆☆☆

Favourite film: ....

Favourite scene: ....

Why: ....

☆☆☆☆☆

Two things that contribute to us not being happy: living in the past and comparing ourselves to others. So let go of what you can't change and take only the lessons away; focus on yourself and don't ever worry about the pace that anyone else is moving at.

MY JOURNAL

Date: ....

Three things I'm proud I accomplished this week:

1 >> ....

....

2 >> ....

....

3 >> ....

....

What was the best day of the week and why? ....

....

....

....

What was the most challenging day of the week and why? ....

....

....

....

This week I was inspired by: ....
....

If I could relive any moment from this week, which one would it be and why?
....
....
....

Favourite quote of the week: ....
....
....

Favourite thing I hinched this week: ....
....
....

Three things to look forward to next week:
♥ ....
♥ ....
♥ ....

MY WEEKLY HINCH LIST

HINCH LIST *continued*

☐
☐
☐
☐
☐
☐
☐
☐

☐
☐
☐
☐
☐
☐
☐
☐

HINCH HAUL

☐
☐
☐
☐
☐
☐
☐
☐
☐

☐
☐
☐
☐
☐
☐
☐
☐
☐

Help Sophie!

Help me find my way to my favourite Zoflora!

Answer on page 287

Plan Your Me-Time

What better way to relax and unwind than to indulge in a whole evening of me-time. As much as we make sure to take amazing care of the people that we love, it's so important that we try and make ourselves a priority too. When we make plans to see our friends, we always make sure to show up. And we shouldn't treat ourselves any differently. It's too easy to say we're going to make more time for ourselves, but never get round to it. Well, today, Hinchers, I'm going to ask you to make a date with yourself, and actually stick to it!

DATE: ....

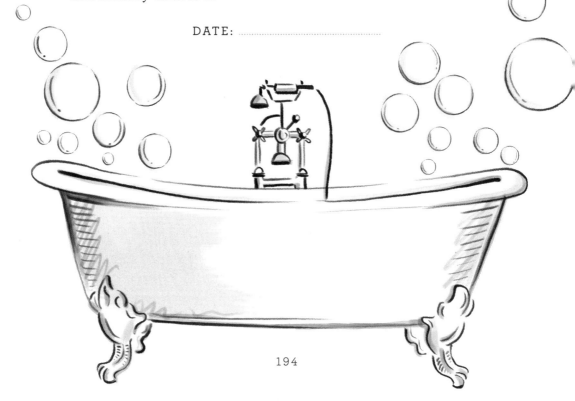

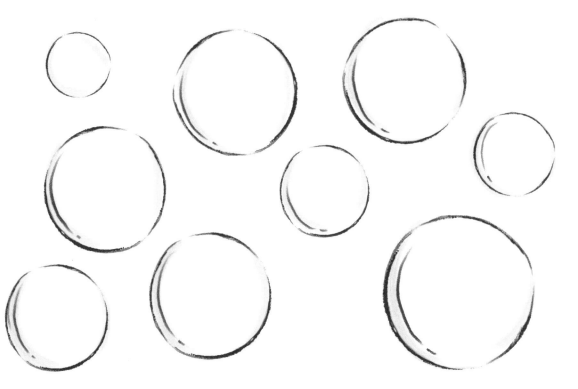

Plan your me-time evening by picking the words below that would make up your idea of the most amazing, relaxing night in and writing them in the bubbles. Add in anything you would love that I've missed! And enjoy!

- [ ] Wax melts
- [ ] Candles
- [ ] Pillow spray
- [ ] Fake tan
- [ ] Face mask
- [ ] Loungewear
- [ ] Read a book/magazine
- [ ] Soak in the bath
- [ ] Nails

- [ ] Hair mask
- [ ] Snacks
- [ ] Sleep
- [ ] Stretch
- [ ] Breathing exercises
- [ ] Meditation
- [ ] Calm app exercise
- [ ] Rain sounds
- [ ] Cosy fleece blanket

The Category Challenge

Fill in the blanks with words that begin with the letter

H

Shop name	....
Author	....
Celebrity	....
Cleaning product	....
Flower	....
Car model	....
Dog breed	....
Country	....
Item of clothing	....
Fruit	....
Insect	....
Something cold	....
Body part	....
Animal	....
Household item	....
Hobby	....
Spice or herb	....
Restaurant	....
Occupation	....
Something that makes you smile	....

The 'Let It Go' Balloons

Sometimes we can get swept up in worrying about things we cannot change and have absolutely no control over. If I start feeling nervous about something, I have to remind myself that worrying doesn't change the outcome. Whether you fret about something or not, if it's going to happen, it's going to happen – and more often than not I've found myself fearing the worst for absolutely no reason at all. What a waste! I love the idea of these balloons! Write your worries in them and let them go. How freeing is that!

Get In Charge Of Your Phone

As you all know, I love my phone. It literally feels like my Hinchers are my best friends and my phone lets us all stay connected with each other, which means the absolute world to me. I just love being able to talk to you and laugh with you through my DMs, and see all of your amazing posts that you tag me in, and enjoy your stories… It's the best. I think, though, that we spend so much time on our phones these days, we sometimes forget to stop and just take in the moment and be present. We can all be guilty of wanting to record a special time so much that we forget to actually live in that moment and fully experience it. A lot of you ask me about where I take Henry for a walk because it's not something I always show you on my stories. He has his favourite field, and when we go there together I like to switch off from the world and use that time to be with my boy, and gather my thoughts, and just enjoy whatever is around me. It's my quiet space. And I think it's really good for us to just switch off from time to time.

SO, HERE IS A LITTLE EXERCISE THAT CAN HELP YOU TO GET A BIT OF SPACE FROM YOUR PHONE…

★ Decide the times you're going to check your phone and try your best to stick to those times. You're going to struggle at first, but don't worry about that. Be strong!

★ Any other time? Don't! Just think: Not now!

★ Do this even if it pings – most things can wait, right?

★ The more you practise ignoring your phone, the better you'll get at it.

And soon, you won't find yourself automatically reaching for your phone! Do something else as a distraction technique to get you out of the habit.

TODAY, WHEN I FEEL LIKE LOOKING AT MY PHONE I'M GOING TO...

☐ Read a magazine

☐ Wipe a surface

☐ Make a cup of tea

☐ Go outside

ADD SOME THINGS YOU THINK YOU COULD DISTRACT YOURSELF WITH BELOW:

....

....

....

....

....

....

....

....

....

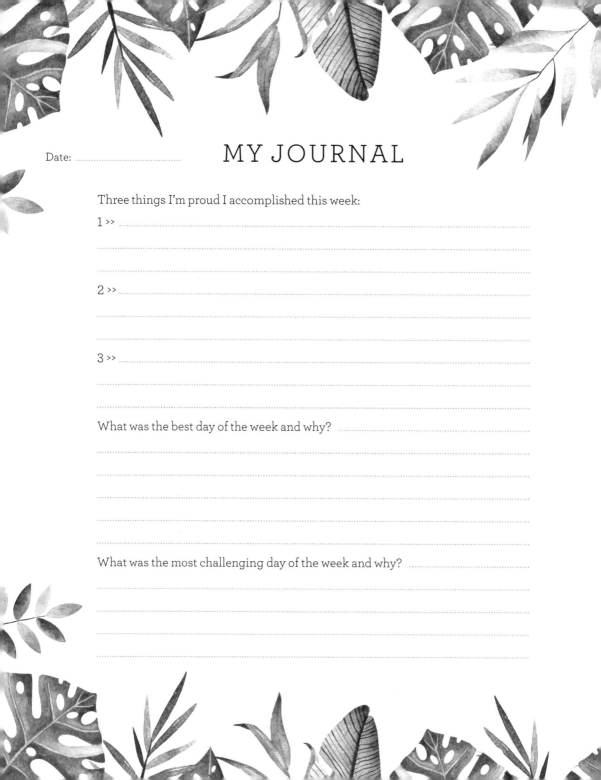

MY JOURNAL

Date: ....

Three things I'm proud I accomplished this week:

1 >> ....
....
....

2 >> ....
....
....

3 >> ....
....

What was the best day of the week and why? ....
....
....
....

What was the most challenging day of the week and why? ....
....
....
....

This week I was inspired by: ....
....
....

If I could relive any moment from this week, which one would it be and why?
....
....
....
....

Favourite quote of the week: ....
....
....

Favourite thing I hinched this week: ....
....
....

Three things to look forward to next week:
♥ ....
....

♥ ....
....

♥ ....
....

Date: ....

MY WEEKLY HINCH LIST

HINCH LIST *continued*

- [ ]
- [ ]
- [ ]
- [ ]
- [ ]
- [ ]
- [ ]
- [ ]

- [ ]
- [ ]
- [ ]
- [ ]
- [ ]
- [ ]
- [ ]
- [ ]

HINCH HAUL

- [ ]
- [ ]
- [ ]
- [ ]
- [ ]
- [ ]
- [ ]
- [ ]
- [ ]

- [ ]
- [ ]
- [ ]
- [ ]
- [ ]
- [ ]
- [ ]
- [ ]
- [ ]

Don't forget to share your hinch lists!

#mrshinchtheactivityjournal

CLEANING
THIS *or* THAT

Underline your fave from each pair!

Zoflora Lavender Escape ⟷ Zoflora Springtime

Lenor Spring Awakening ⟷ Lenor Gold Orchid

Harpic Fresh Mountain Pine ⟷ Harpic Orchid Bloom

Bloo Ocean Mist ⟷ Bloo Rose & Apple Blossom

Dettol Crisp Linen ⟷ Dettol Orchard Blossom

Cif Lemon Cream ⟷ Cif Pink Flower Cream

1001 Thai Orchid ⟷ 1001 Fresh Linen

Febreze Blossom & Breeze ⟷ Febreze Cotton Fresh

Fairy Original ⟷ Fairy Platinum

Unstoppables Lavish ⟷ Unstoppables Fresh

I'd love to see your choices on Instagram, Hinchers! Don't
forget to share and **#mrshinchtheactivityjournal**, and why
not upload a blank copy so your friends can join in too!

Relive A Favourite Memory

It's easy to forget the happy times, Hinchers, when you are overwhelmed with the stresses of everyday life. For this activity I'd like you to find some time in your day when you can sit down and stare into space and really think about some of the happiest times you've ever had, whether they were on your own, with a loved one or in a big group. Moments when you were really proud of yourself, feeling loved up, or just properly loving life!

HERE ARE SOME OF MINE:

1» Picking Henry up and bringing him home for the first time

2» Collecting the keys to our very first home that we saved up so long to buy

3» Marrying the love of my life, Jamie

4» Holding the first copy of *Hinch Yourself Happy*

5» Holding my darling boy, Ronnie, in my arms for the first time

NOW IT'S YOUR TURN TO REMINISCE AWAY...

1»

2»

3»

4»

5»

The Five Senses Challenge

Life can sometimes feel very overwhelming. One way that can be effective to help you to feel calm, particularly in a moment of panic, is to try and centre your focus on your surroundings as a bit of a distraction. Pay proper attention to what is around you. Have a go at this challenge by taking a deep breath and writing down the answers to the five questions below:

Write down FIVE things you can see:

1 » .... 4 » ....

2 » .... 5 » ....

3 » ....

Write down FOUR things you can touch:

1 » .... 3 » ....

2 » .... 4 » ....

Write down THREE things you can hear:

1 » .... 3 » ....

2 » ....

Write down TWO things you can smell:

1 » .... 2 » ....

Write down ONE thing you can taste:

1 » ....

Favourite Music

List your favourite artists, albums and favourite song on said album.

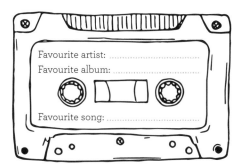

Favourite artist: ....
Favourite album: ....

Favourite song: ....

Favourite artist: ....
Favourite album: ....

Favourite song: ....

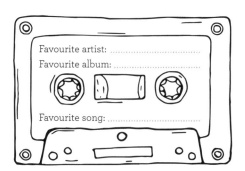

Favourite artist: ....
Favourite album: ....

Favourite song: ....

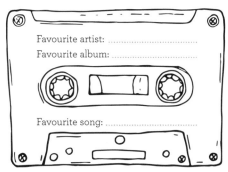

Favourite artist: ....
Favourite album: ....

Favourite song: ....

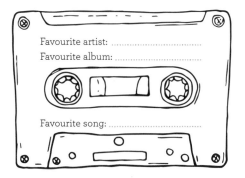

Favourite artist: ....
Favourite album: ....

Favourite song: ....

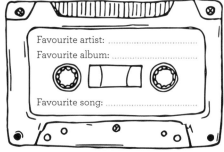

Favourite artist: ....
Favourite album: ....

Favourite song: ....

Cut The Clutter

As you would in a Clockwise Clean, start at the door and work your way around each room in your house until you get back to the entrance. Using these pretty frames, label whichever room you're in and identify the areas you think could do with a declutter. Examples for me would include: my Tupperware cupboard in the kitchen and my ottoman in the lounge. Once you have all of your lists written up, work out a plan of action for when you're going to tackle each area. Remember to make the plan manageable and realistic, because the last thing we need is to add to our already very busy to-do lists! So try and have a go at slowly making your way through your plan as and when you've got some spare time, ticking each item off as you go, and you'll be amazed at the progress you're making! Tidy house, tidy mind!

Reasons To Be Grateful Check-In

Okay, it's time to count your blessings again! This page is all about taking a moment to think about all your reasons to be thankful. Please write below five new things you are grateful for today:

1 » ....

2 » ....

3 » ....

4 » ....

5 » ....

We all go through tough times, and you may be dealing with some difficult things at the moment. If you are, please write down three challenges you are currently facing, and anything you've learnt from them:

1 » ....

....

2 » ....

....

....

3 » ....

....

....

You have to fight through some bad days
to earn the best days of your life. ♡

Everything will make sense someday. So for now, laugh at your mistakes, smile through the tears and keep reminding yourself that everything really does happen for a reason.

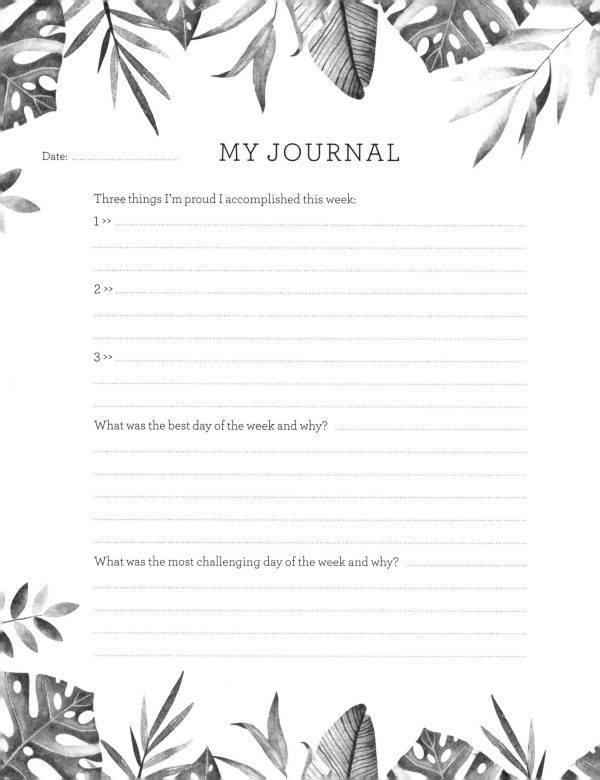

Date: ....

MY JOURNAL

Three things I'm proud I accomplished this week:

1 >> ....

....

....

2 >> ....

....

....

3 >> ....

....

....

What was the best day of the week and why? ....

....

....

....

....

What was the most challenging day of the week and why? ....

....

....

....

....

This week I was inspired by: ....
....

If I could relive any moment from this week, which one would it be and why?
....
....
....

Favourite quote of the week: ....
....
....

Favourite thing I hinched this week: ....
....
....

Three things to look forward to next week:
♥ ....
....
♥ ....
....
♥ ....
....

Date: ....

MY WEEKLY HINCH LIST

HINCH LIST *continued*

- [ ]
- [ ]
- [ ]
- [ ]
- [ ]
- [ ]
- [ ]
- [ ]
- [ ]

- [ ]
- [ ]
- [ ]
- [ ]
- [ ]
- [ ]
- [ ]
- [ ]
- [ ]

- [ ]
- [ ]
- [ ]
- [ ]
- [ ]
- [ ]
- [ ]
- [ ]
- [ ]

HINCH HAUL

- [ ]
- [ ]
- [ ]
- [ ]
- [ ]
- [ ]
- [ ]
- [ ]
- [ ]

How quickly can you unscramble these Hincher favourites?
Fill in the blanks with the unscrambled words.

1. chin hilts   _ _ _ _ _ / _ _ _ _

HINT: Love to tick this off!

2. ad puffin sherry   _ _ _ _ _ ' _ / _ _ / _ _ _ _ _ _

HINT: Time to get ready for the weekend . . .

3. hila hnuch   _ _ _ _ _ / _ _ _ _

HINT: What I love to do in B&M.

4. mewls tax   _ _ _ / _ _ _ _ _

HINT: Which one will I choose tonight?

5. air nan   _ _ _ _ _ _

HINT: The most magical place on earth if you ask me!

6. chin hams   _ _ _ _ _ _ _ _

HINT: 'Tis the season . . .

7. lowibse leverages   _ _ _ _ _ / _ _ _ _ _ / _ _ _ _ _ _

HINT: He does the work so you don't have to . . .

8. hartshorn shake   _ _ _ _ _ _ / _ _ _ / _ _ _ _ _

HINT: Great for my carpets!

9. elsy grog grove   _ _ _ _ _ _ _ / _ _ _ _ _ _

HINT: A hinching essential.

10. achiest blob   _ _ _ _ _ / _ _ _ _ _ _

HINT: They all have their own names.

Answers on page 287

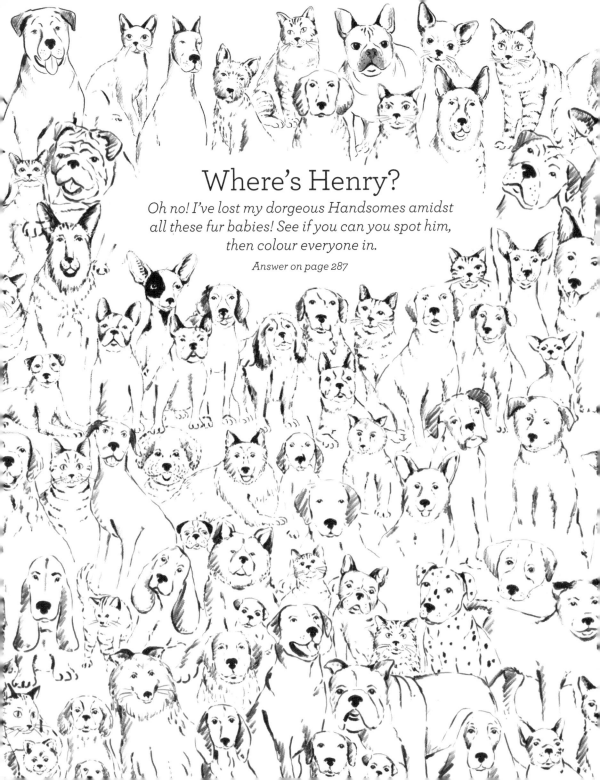

Where's Henry?

Oh no! I've lost my dorgeous Handsomes amidst all these fur babies! See if you can you spot him, then colour everyone in.

Answer on page 287

Mind Map

I love using these little diagrams to come up with ideas or to make notes on a certain subject – home improvements or holiday planning, for example. You can be really creative, as you're not worrying about putting things in a certain order – you can just let your mind roam free! Write your main subject in the middle circle and then work from there.

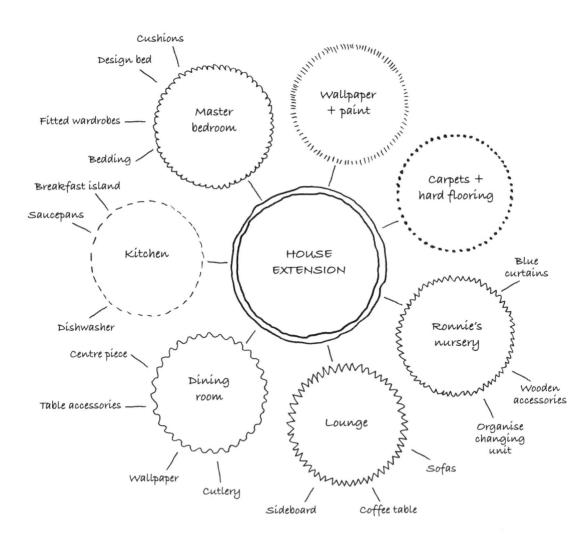

Now you fill in yours!

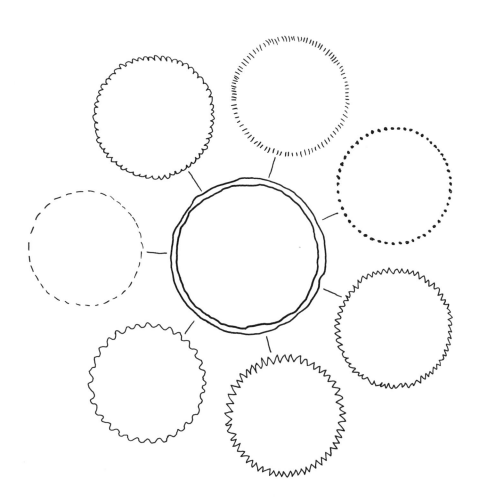

Sudoku Fun

Fill in the missing squares!

HINCH HINT: Each large square must contain the numbers
1 to 9. Each column and row must also contain the numbers 1 to 9.

8		7	2		3			
		2		7	9			
						7		
7							6	2
3		1						5
	4		8					
	9		6	4				8
3		1				2		
7	4	6		3	2			9

Answers on page 287

Those Odd Jobs

Right, Hinchers, there's always those odd jobs around the house that you keep putting off. It took me so long to motivate myself to hinch my wardrobe, but once it was done it felt so good.

So let's free your mind of those odd jobs you've not yet got around to completing. Write them below and give yourself a date to get them done by. You'll feel so much better once they are hinched!

Odd job: *Organise my wardrobe*
Completion date: *by Friday 17th!*
Action plan: *Buy some coat hangers, get some vacuum storage bags and drawer dividers. Take unwanted clothes to the charity shop.*

Odd job 1:
Completion date:
Action plan:

Odd job 2:
Completion date:
Action plan:

Odd job 3:
Completion date:
Action plan:

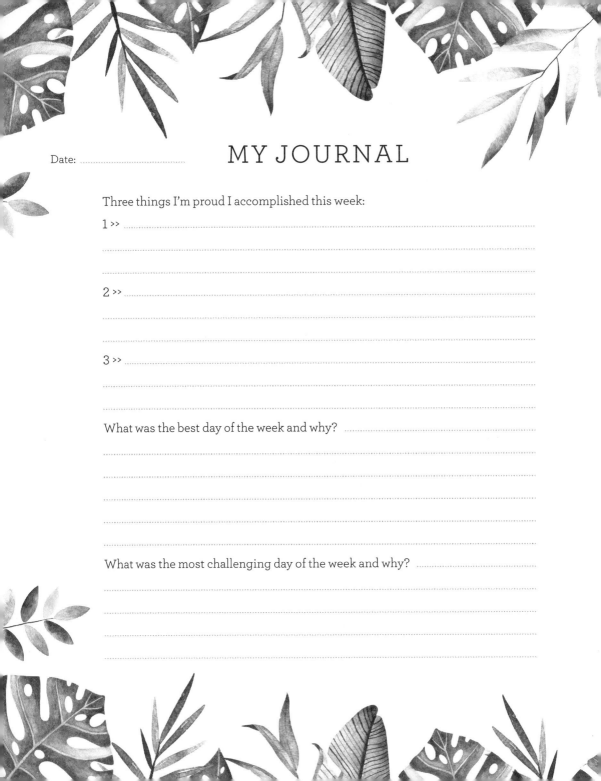

MY JOURNAL

Date: ....

Three things I'm proud I accomplished this week:

1 >> ....
....
....

2 >> ....
....
....

3 >> ....
....
....

What was the best day of the week and why? ....
....
....
....
....

What was the most challenging day of the week and why? ....
....
....
....

This week I was inspired by: ....
....

If I could relive any moment from this week, which one would it be and why?
....
....
....

Favourite quote of the week: ....
....
....

Favourite thing I hinched this week: ....
....
....

Three things to look forward to next week:
♥ ....

♥ ....

♥ ....
....

MY WEEKLY HINCH LIST

HINCH LIST *continued*

☐

☐

☐

☐

☐

☐

☐

☐

☐

☐

☐

☐

☐

☐

☐

☐

☐

☐

HINCH HAUL

☐

☐

☐

☐

☐

☐

☐

☐

☐

☐

☐

☐

☐

☐

☐

☐

☐

☐

I'd love to see your hinch lists!

#mrshinchtheactivityjournal

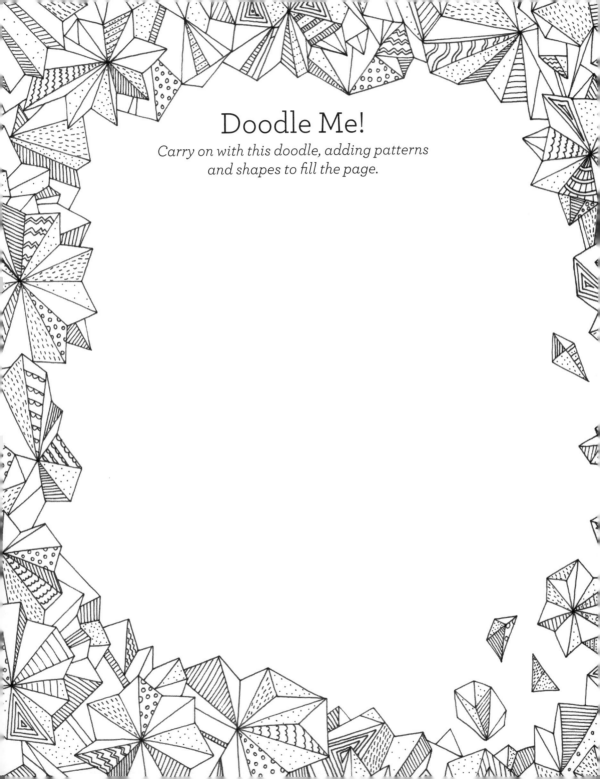

Doodle Me!

Carry on with this doodle, adding patterns and shapes to fill the page.

Coming Home

I'm always so happy to get back to my home, no matter where I've been or how much of a good time I've had out. As you will have seen, there are a few things I do before leaving the house to make coming home that much more familiar and homely. There's nothing quite like stepping back through the door to the fresh smell of a pined loo and a Minkeh-soaked Zoflora sink! Incredible! I've noticed I follow the same sort of routine when I get in from being out, and that little ritual sets me up for my best evenings.

First things first, I've always got to make a fuss of Handsomes Henry. He doesn't give you much choice really but I just love it so much. He sits on his step at the bottom of the stairs and makes the most adorable noises ready for his ear rubs. I like to think he's talking to Mumma and telling me all about the time I've missed. Which is usually about two hours max but if you ask Henry, he'll make it sound like it's been all day. Oh dear Dorgeous!

Next, the hair goes up and I like to lose whatever clothes I'm wearing and throw on a soft, comfy lounge set of some kind. I'd absolutely live in them if I could! They're the best. Then it's Ava May time! I'll have a wander around the house and light all my wax melts for the evening to make everything nice and cosy. I can't be the only one who looks forward to new wax melt day! I just love going through my basket and picking which scent I'm going to change all the melts to. Heaven! I then empty the sinks of Zoflora and have a quick spray of the kitchen counter tops, and we're ready to start our evening!

WHAT COULD YOU DO TO MAKE COMING HOME AFTER A BUSY DAY THAT MUCH NICER?

Natural Highs

You know I'm not exactly known for my love of exercise. All the best! Some of my favourite times, which you don't see a lot of because I like to use them as quiet times to think and reflect, are when I take Henry on a walk. Between Mr Hinch and me, Handsomes goes out on an adventure at least twice a day, and I honestly love it when it's my turn to take him, especially to his favourite field. It's well known that being in the fresh air is an instant mood lifter, and can be really good for your mental health. I have definitely noticed how much better I feel once I've taken Dorgeous out, and I know how much he loves it too!

It's not just that walking itself is great exercise. There's also loads of proof now that being close to nature – even if that's just a tree or a patch of grass – is good for you.

SIMPLE WAYS TO MAKE SURE YOU GET OUTSIDE MORE:

★ A little does the job. Even having a tiny bit of nature in your day helps you relax – seeing a tree, the sky, even hearing birds. So go and open one of your windows, and just look outside!

★ It's even better, obviously, if you can go outside! Even if it's just for 20 minutes a day. You've seen how much I love having a potter in the garden. Even if I don't end up doing very much, just being outside feels amazing.

★ You can get the benefits by bringing nature inside too, whether with a bunch of flowers or a lovely plant (Keith!).

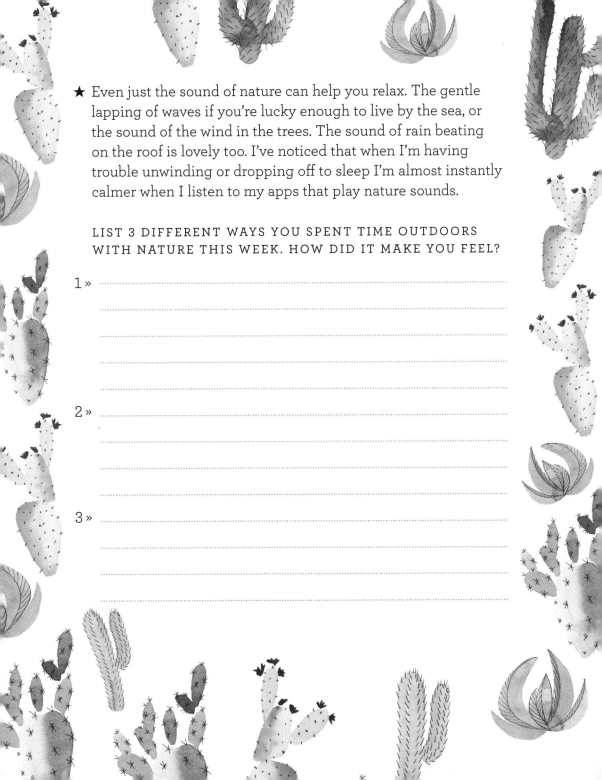

★ Even just the sound of nature can help you relax. The gentle lapping of waves if you're lucky enough to live by the sea, or the sound of the wind in the trees. The sound of rain beating on the roof is lovely too. I've noticed that when I'm having trouble unwinding or dropping off to sleep I'm almost instantly calmer when I listen to my apps that play nature sounds.

LIST 3 DIFFERENT WAYS YOU SPENT TIME OUTDOORS WITH NATURE THIS WEEK. HOW DID IT MAKE YOU FEEL?

1 »

2 »

3 »

The Category Challenge

Fill in the blanks with words that begin with the letter

E

Shop name	
Author	
Celebrity	
Cleaning product	
Flower	
Car model	
Dog breed	
Country	
Item of clothing	
Fruit	
Insect	
Something cold	
Body part	
Animal	
Household item	
Hobby	
Spice or herb	
Restaurant	
Occupation	
Something that makes you smile	

Try not to compare yourself to others. YOU are amazing and that's all that matters.

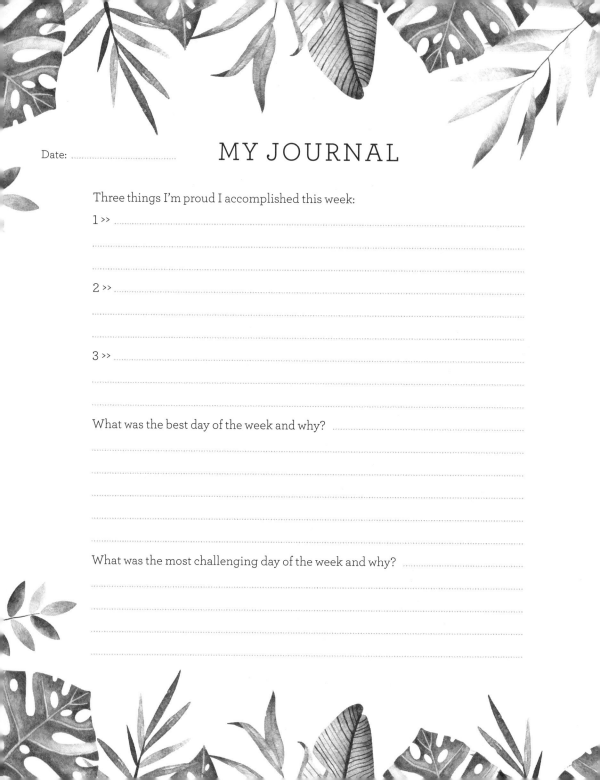

Date: ....

MY JOURNAL

Three things I'm proud I accomplished this week:

1 >> ....

....

....

2 >> ....

....

....

3 >> ....

....

....

What was the best day of the week and why? ....

....

....

....

....

What was the most challenging day of the week and why? ....

....

....

....

....

This week I was inspired by: ....
....

If I could relive any moment from this week, which one would it be and why?
....
....
....
....

Favourite quote of the week: ....
....
....
....

Favourite thing I hinched this week: ....
....
....
....

Three things to look forward to next week:
♥ ....
....
♥ ....
....
♥ ....
....

MY WEEKLY HINCH LIST

HINCH LIST *continued*

☐

☐

☐

☐

☐

☐

☐

☐

☐

☐

☐

☐

☐

☐

☐

☐

HINCH HAUL

☐

☐

☐

☐

☐

☐

☐

☐

☐

☐

☐

☐

☐

☐

☐

☐

☐

☐

Sophie's Baskets

I'd be lost without my baskets. Use this page to plan some helpful baskets of your own. They could be for anything – cleaning products, cosmetics, toiletries – whatever it would be helpful to organise. Please just write them down here first and then go and create your baskets in real life. I promise that once you've tried baskets you won't go back!

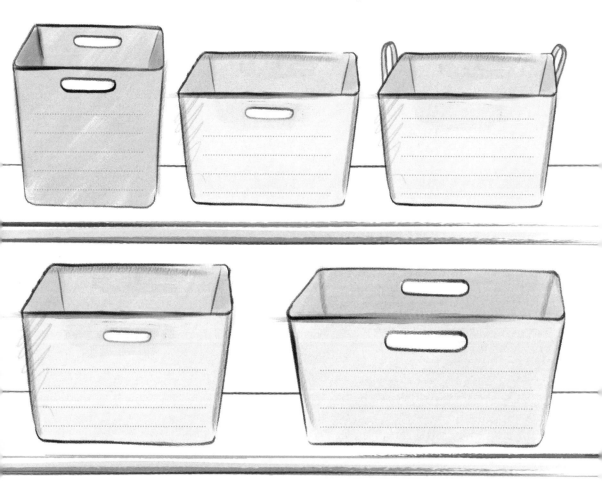

DOT-TO-DOT

Don't forget to colour me in afterwards!

Answers on page 288

Hinching Tools Word Search

Can you spot some of our favourite family members?

```
F O L E Y C R T I V N Z H A R L Q E C Z T B T V D
R E C E O D T W M V R F K M S G T D W V U I L D W
B K W L J P D G M Q P U P V D I S J Y F M R J K A
N A I R B B T U X W X I Z G A P W A F R U A N J Y
K F A D J Q B J B C V S W I B O C T E R B Z V I F
E E T A V J W J P T C A X G M V I K P L A H V L R
P A P A I S C Y M Z N I M M Q N I K F U R N O L Z
Y E L L E H S Y W F Z K G D G B H C Y W R G E I I
V E G P C N D O O H I N J S A Z H E T R Y D P I A
I Q L E L C O K S C R U B D A D D Y K O O Q Q Q L
C E S X C D Q Q J L B V T O C N P S Y N R G L Q M
F D I J C A H R B W J I K M P N Z M C N I S E S K
A D E J N T R H F S J X H E X P D B O N J M I R H
S M C Y B O Q T H N E H Z M R F M R T M O Q A S G
Y P B A C G D D D F B B H B A E A Y P N N U G G R
H V W I S Y E T T I W K U L V H D A V B I J Z L W
A E J G Q K J G W F S A N W S K H R U X V W Z Z Y
N D K C Z L O S T E W A R T V H M A Z A G D C T U
N Q K N X N W Z J N Y Z A A X B B B X H Y F L T E
I U E J I O U F E L L R H Z A X T R J A V L A T L
K Z V X D P V L U N E P P D O X W A E B U H R S V
K X F J T M B S L V H Y D D Q C Q B B T I H E Z R
M H N E V A B S C V C M H Y Y L D J S A Y T N E I
L E N N I E O B B B T K I I R N P A O K X P C V W
D V K W K U O N B X B V G K M W D A V E R M E O L
```

- ☐ Derek
- ☐ Buff Tings
- ☐ Pinkeh
- ☐ Minkeh
- ☐ Barry
- ☐ Kermit
- ☐ Neil
- ☐ Gregory
- ☐ Shelley
- ☐ Sharon
- ☐ Stewart
- ☐ Buddy
- ☐ Brian
- ☐ Barbara
- ☐ Vera
- ☐ Trace
- ☐ Victor
- ☐ Scrub Daddy
- ☐ Dave
- ☐ Clarence
- ☐ Lennie

Answers on page 288

Favourite TV Shows

List your favourite TV shows, best episode from each show and why in the TV screens below. These can be of all time, or ones you've been loving lately. It's up to you!

Favourite show: ....

Favourite episode: ....

Why: ....

....

....

....

Favourite show: ....

Favourite episode: ....

Why: ....

....

....

....

Favourite show: ....

Favourite episode: ....

Why: ....

....

....

....

Favourite show: ....

Favourite episode: ....

Why: ....

....

....

....

Favourite show: ....

Favourite episode: ....

Why: ....

....

....

....

Favourite show: ....

Favourite episode: ....

Why: ....

....

....

....

What Makes Me Happy

*Circle the things that make you happy and
draw in any others that you like!*

Exercise

Fur babies

Hinching

Friends

Tea

Instagram

Minkeh!

Pizza

Rainbows

Mums

Baths

TV

Books

Garden

Flowers

Cushions

Fields

Romance

Memories

Sleep

Seasons

Baskets

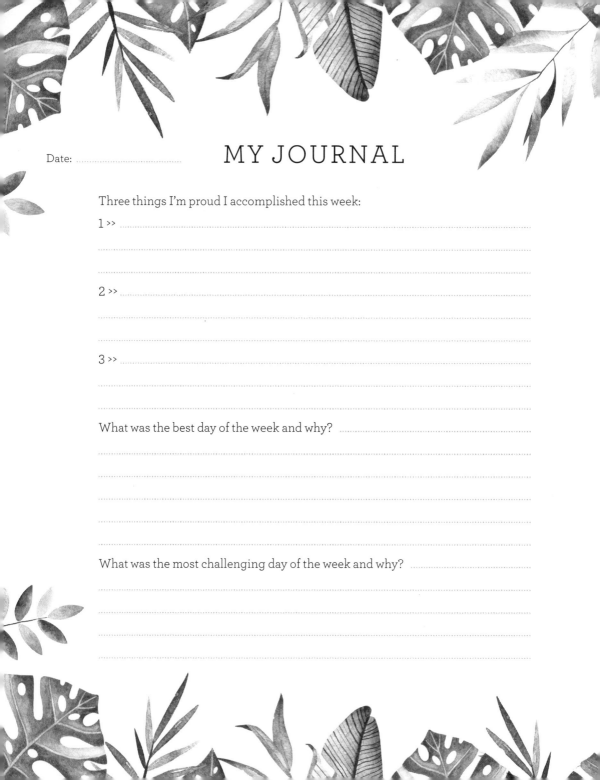

MY JOURNAL

Date: ....

Three things I'm proud I accomplished this week:

1 >> ....
....
....

2 >> ....
....
....

3 >> ....
....
....

What was the best day of the week and why? ....
....
....
....
....

What was the most challenging day of the week and why? ....
....
....
....

This week I was inspired by: ....
....

If I could relive any moment from this week, which one would it be and why?
....
....
....

Favourite quote of the week: ....
....
....

Favourite thing I hinched this week: ....
....
....

Three things to look forward to next week:
♥ ....
♥ ....
♥ ....

Date: ....

MY WEEKLY HINCH LIST

- [ ]
- [ ]
- [ ]
- [ ]
- [ ]
- [ ]
- [ ]
- [ ]

- [ ]
- [ ]
- [ ]
- [ ]
- [ ]
- [ ]
- [ ]
- [ ]

HINCH HAUL

- [ ]
- [ ]
- [ ]
- [ ]
- [ ]
- [ ]
- [ ]
- [ ]
- [ ]

- [ ]
- [ ]
- [ ]
- [ ]
- [ ]
- [ ]
- [ ]
- [ ]
- [ ]

Don't forget to share your hinch lists!

#mrshinchtheactivityjournal

A Laugh A Day...

What's the point of life if you can't have a laugh, especially at yourself? Me and my Hinchers laugh together every day. Sometimes I'll laugh so hard, people might think I've lost it! Identify the things that make you laugh – and try and do as many of them as you can!

THESE ARE THREE THINGS THAT NEVER FAIL TO MAKE ME LAUGH:

★ Believe it or not – Jamie! He makes me cry with laughter, without fail, every day!

★ My eBayers – I think we all can tell by now that I have a bit of an eBay addiction. And, as I show you, I have had some cracking fails that crease me up!

★ Tracy – we speak every day, and she has me laughing so much that it actually makes my tummy physically hurt. I just love her.

NOW WRITE DOWN THINGS THAT NEVER FAIL TO CRACK YOU UP:

3 things that last made me laugh:

1. ....

2. ....

3. ....

3 people who always make me laugh:

1. ....

2. ....

3. ....

Most embarrassing moment: ....

....

Don't worry – I have so many of these!

THINGS TO EAT AND DRINK
THIS *or* THAT

Underline your fave from each pair!

Avocado toast ⟷ Bacon sandwich

Sunday roast ⟷ Fish and chips

Burger and chips ⟷ Mac and cheese

Pizza ⟷ Lasagne

Curry ⟷ Chinese

Salad ⟷ Soup

Apple crumble ⟷ Sticky toffee pudding

Magnum ⟷ Cornetto

Tea ⟷ Coffee

Wine ⟷ Gin

Haribo ⟷ Dairy Milk

Doritos ⟷ Kettle Chips

I'd love to see your choices on Instagram, Hinchers! Don't
forget to share and **#mrshinchtheactivityjournal**, and why
not upload a blank copy so your friends can join in too!

Help Henry!

Handsomes needs to find his birthday cake.
Can you help him through the maze?

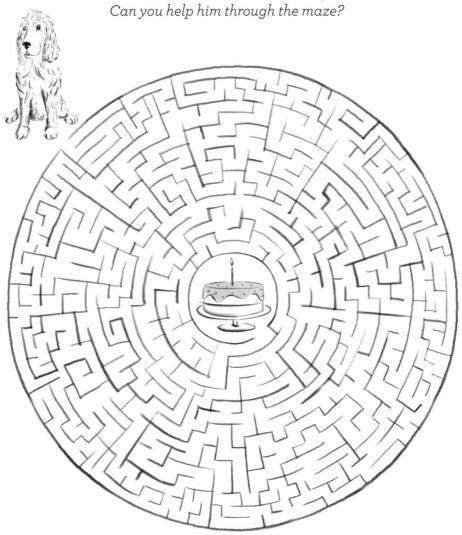

Answer on page 288

Goal Check-In

Goal 1 Review

Please go back to page 19 and check your first goal.

My goal»

What things have you already done to progress your goal?

1»

2»

3»

What have been your biggest obstacles so far?

1»

2»

3»

List some things that you still need to do to achieve your goal:

1»

2»

3»

Goal 2 Review

Please go back to page 20 and check your second goal.

My goal» ....

What things have you already done to progress your goal?

1» ....

2» ....

3» ....

What have been your biggest obstacles so far?

1» ....

2» ....

3» ....

List some things that you still need to do to achieve your goal:

1» ....

2» ....

3» ....

Goal 3 Review

Please go back to page 21 and check your third goal.

My goal» ....

What things have you already done to progress your goal?

1» ....

2» ....

3» ....

What have been your biggest obstacles so far?

1» ....

2» ....

3» ....

List some things that you still need to do to achieve your goal:

1» ....

2» ....

3» ....

DREAM BIG,
You CAN make it happen

MY JOURNAL

Date: ....

Three things I'm proud I accomplished this week:

1 >> ....

....

....

2 >> ....

....

....

3 >> ....

....

What was the best day of the week and why? ....

....

....

....

What was the most challenging day of the week and why? ....

....

....

....

This week I was inspired by: ....

....

If I could relive any moment from this week, which one would it be and why?

....

....

....

....

Favourite quote of the week: ....

....

....

....

Favourite thing I hinched this week: ....

....

....

....

Three things to look forward to next week:

♥ ....

....

♥ ....

....

♥ ....

....

Date: ....

MY WEEKLY HINCH LIST

HINCH LIST *continued*

- [ ]
- [ ]
- [ ]
- [ ]
- [ ]
- [ ]
- [ ]
- [ ]
- [ ]

- [ ]
- [ ]
- [ ]
- [ ]
- [ ]
- [ ]
- [ ]
- [ ]
- [ ]

HINCH HAUL

- [ ]
- [ ]
- [ ]
- [ ]
- [ ]
- [ ]
- [ ]
- [ ]
- [ ]

- [ ]
- [ ]
- [ ]
- [ ]
- [ ]
- [ ]
- [ ]
- [ ]
- [ ]

The Category Challenge

Fill in the blanks with words that begin with the letter

R

Shop name ....

Author ....

Celebrity ....

Cleaning product ....

Flower ....

Car model ....

Dog breed ....

Country ....

Item of clothing ....

Fruit ....

Insect ....

Something cold ....

Body part ....

Animal ....

Household item ....

Hobby ....

Spice or herb ....

Restaurant ....

Occupation ....

Something that
makes you smile ....

Secret Garden

*Colour in this beautiful, peaceful
garden. Don't forget to share and*
#mrshinchtheactivityjournal

Hinch Your Sudoku

Fill in the missing squares!

HINCH HINT: Fill the grid with the four
hinching objects so that each object is only used
once in each row, column and 2×2 block.

Answers on page 288

Reasons To Be Grateful Check-In

Okay, here is our third and final gratitude page in the book. As you know by now, I think taking a moment to be thankful is one of the best things you can do in life. It reminds us what really matters. Please write below five new things you are grateful for today:

1 » ....

2 » ....

3 » ....

4 » ....

5 » ....

Now we're nearing the end of this little book, I'd like you to have a think about which pages have been your favourites. I always find that when life is getting on top of me, there's no better way to calm my mind than putting pen to paper and writing a little list. I hope that you have found some peace of mind and a little bit of me-time in this book. I sincerely hope some of the activities have helped you. Please list the three you found most beneficial here:

1 » ....

....

2 » ....

....

3 » ....

....

Gratitude turns what we have into enough.

The Power Of Saying Yes

It's all too easy to spend our lives constantly turning down invitations and saying no to new experiences that are outside of our comfort zones. You know me, Hinchers. I'm a homebody. Give me a comfy lounge set and a pair of slippers over going out, any day of the week! But sometimes...just sometimes...saying yes to things can bring about the most amazing twists and turns in our lives, and the most unexpected, incredible surprises. Just look at me now! All of this craziness has happened so fast! And whilst I'm just taking each new day as it comes, and seeing what new surprise is waiting for me around each corner, I've become so much more open to saying yes to opportunities, because you never ever know where they may lead!

Have a think about 3 things outside of your comfort zone that you're going to say yes to, and write them below:

1»

2»

3»

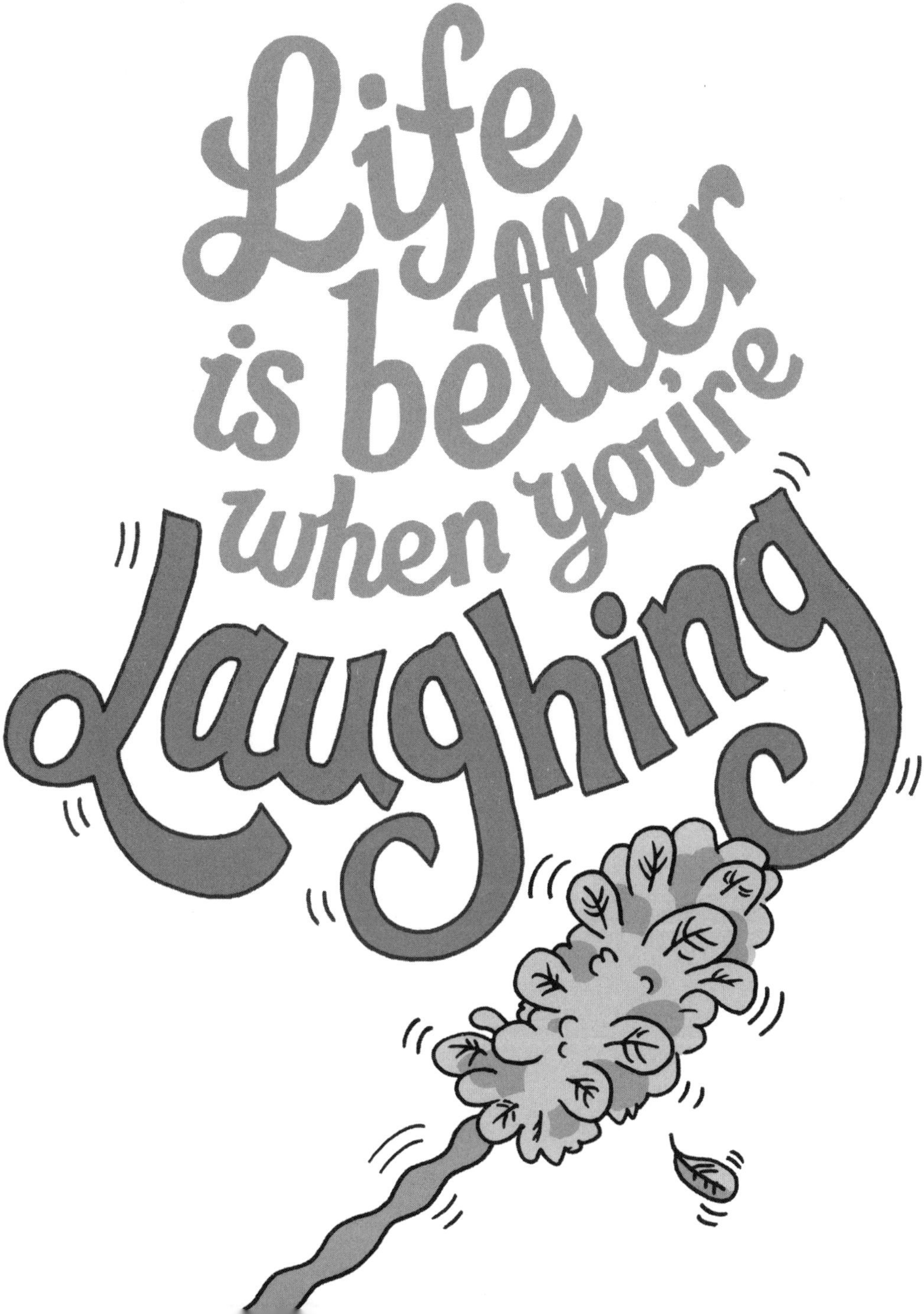
Life is better when you're laughing

MY JOURNAL

Date: ....

Three things I'm proud I accomplished this week:

1 >> ....

....

....

2 >> ....

....

....

3 >> ....

....

....

What was the best day of the week and why? ....

....

....

....

....

What was the most challenging day of the week and why? ....

....

....

....

....

This week I was inspired by: ....

....

If I could relive any moment from this week, which one would it be and why?

....

....

....

Favourite quote of the week: ....

....

....

Favourite thing I hinched this week: ....

....

....

Three things to look forward to next week:

♥ ....

♥ ....

♥ ....

You did it, my Hincher!

You stuck with me and smashed it all the way through to the end of your activity journal. I am so proud of you! You've done absolutely amazing!

I hope you enjoyed completing your book as much as I loved putting it together for you. I really hope it's managed to help you in some way; be it by giving you that much needed time out excuse, or by helping you to organise some of your thoughts a bit more, or maybe even by just putting a big smile on your face. The thought just makes me so happy!

Lots of love,
Soph
xxx

Tadaa!

As I'm sure many of you know, I love a tadaa list – I use them on those days when my hinch lists seem a bit too much, and they help me to record and write down everything I've achieved that day. You usually get so much more done than you'd ever realise, and they're a great way of acknowledging your accomplishments, particularly on those days when you don't feel up to tackling much!

Tadaa!

-
-
-
-
-
-
-
-
-
-
-
-
-
-

XXX

Tadaa!

-
-
-
-
-
-
-
-
-
-
-
-
-
-
-

XXX

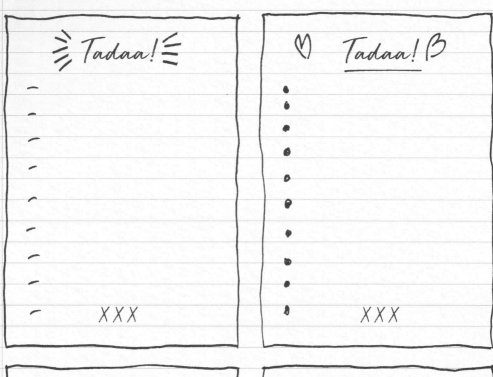

Tadaa!

- —
- —
- —
- —
- —
- —
- —

XXX

Tadaa!

XXX

Tadaa!

XXX

Tadaa!

XXX

Notes...

Notes...

Notes...

Notes...

Answers

Hinchionary Word Search Page 27

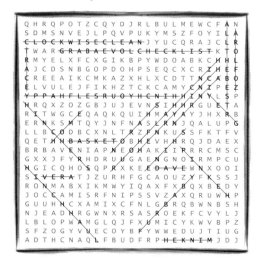

All The Best; Love A Barg; Narnia; Hinch Haul; Vera; Zoflora; Basket; Shine; Fur Baby; Checklist; Hinch Half Hour; Clockwise Clean; Pinkeh; Henry Hinch; Home; Minkeh; Grey; Hinchers; Trace; Dave; Sharon; Hinch Yourself Happy

Finding The Hinching Names Page 43

Barry.....................brushes
Buff Tings.....................mop slippers
Clarence.....................polish cloth
Cliff.....................stainless-steel spray
Dave.....................fluffy duster
Derek.....................Dishmatic
Gregory.....................gloves
Kermit.....................glass and window cloth
Lennie.....................lint roller
Minkeh.....................antibacterial cleaning pad
Neil.....................kneeling pad
Pinkeh.....................moppet sponge
Sharon.....................vacuum cleaner
Stewart.....................sonic scrubber
Trace.....................turbo mop
Vera.....................spray mop
Victor.....................window vacuum

Zoflora Where It All Began Page 36

Lilac	Summer Breeze
Bouquet	Winter Morning
Lavender	Green Valley
Pine	Honeysuckle & Jasmine
Jasmine	Hello Spring
Carnation	Lavender Escape
Lilly Fresh	Cranberry and Orange
Rain Fresh	Warm Cinnamon
Citrus Fresh	Winter Spice
Hyacinth	Sweetpea
Rose	Hello Spring
Springtime	Lavender Escape
Cool & Fresh	Summer Breeze
Wallflower	Bluebell Woods
Flowershop	Mountain Air (Fresh Home)
Cherry Blossom	Winter Morning
Linen Fresh	Mandarin & Lime
Apple Orchard	Summer Berries
Bluebell Woods	Festive Fireside
Summer Bouquet	Tropical Twist
Country Garden	Paradise Peach
Twilight Garden	Lemon Zing
Orchid	Mountain Air (Green Valley)
Oriental Lilly	Secret Garden
Pink Grapefruit	

Where's Minkeh? Page 47

Completed Dot-To-Dot Page 56

Sudoku Fun 1 Page 67

3	7	5	4	2	8	9	1	6
1	6	4	5	3	9	8	7	2
2	9	8	6	1	7	4	3	5
4	5	1	3	8	6	7	2	9
8	2	6	9	7	5	3	4	1
7	3	9	2	4	1	5	6	8
9	1	3	8	6	4	2	5	7
5	4	7	1	9	2	6	8	3
6	8	2	7	5	3	1	9	4

Word Scramble Page 70

1. furl hora zoo .... zoflora hour
2. bees ray .... ebayers
3. biff stung .... buff tings
4. flori hah hcuhn .... hinch half hour
5. knits puff .... pink stuff
6. duvets earthed .... dave the duster
7. hpnike .... pinkeh
8. ins mekon think .... mink on the sink
9. amex pipits .... pixie stamp
10. ballet seth .... all the best

Match The Hinching Product Page 83

Squeegee .... Stairs
Flash Bathroom .... Bathtub
Dave the Duster .... Ornament
Harpic Active Fresh .... Toilet
Zoflora .... Toilet brush
Elbow Grease .... UPVC window frames

283

Crossword Page 79

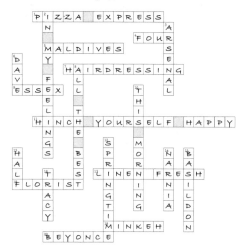

ACROSS: 1. Pizza Express; **4.** Four; **5.** Maldives;
7. Hairdressing; **9.** Essex; **11.** Hinch Yourself Happy;
17. Linen Fresh; **18.** Florist; **19.** Minkeh; **20.** Beyoncé

DOWN: 2. In My Feelings; **3.** Arsenal; **6.** Dave;
8. All The Best; **10.** This Morning; **12.** Springtime;
13. Half; **14.** Narnia **15.** Basildon; **16.** Tracy

Help Henry! Page 91

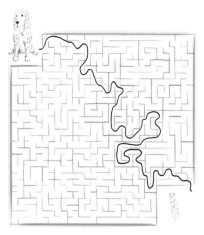

Spot The Difference Pages 92–93

Hinch Your Sudoku Page 115

My Hinching Soundtrack Crossword Page 133

ACROSS:
5. Usher
6. Drake
8. The Boy Is Mine
9. Flawless
10. Elton John

DOWN:
1. Vandross
2. Shark
3. Survivor
4. Whitney Houston
7. Respect

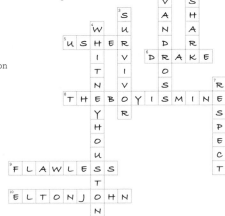

Ava May Wax Melt Scent Word Search Page 148

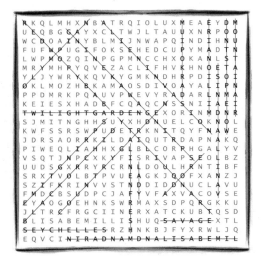

Alien Invasion; Adore; Baby Powder; Black Orchid; Dark Opium; Don't Stop Me Now; Lady; Lime Basil and Mandarin; Millionaire; Olympian; Savage; Seychelles; Spring Awakening; Tranquility; Vanilla and Anise; Linen Fresh; Twilight Garden; Springtime; Country Garden; Mountain Air

Dot-To-Dot Page 159

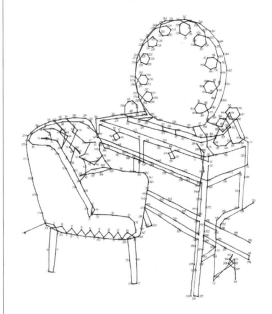

Colour In The Cloth Family Page 169

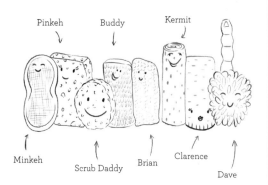

Pinkeh   Buddy   Kermit

Minkeh   Scrub Daddy   Brian   Clarence   Dave

A Few Of My Favourite Things Page 181

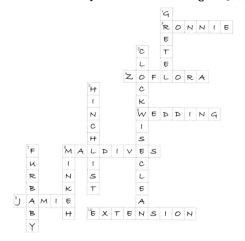

ACROSS:
2. Ronnie
4. Zoflora
6. Wedding
8. Maldives
9. Jamie
10. Extension

DOWN:
1. Gretel
3. Clockwise Clean
5. Hinch list
7. Fur baby
8. Minkeh

Spot The Difference Page 173

Where's Sophie? Pages 184–185

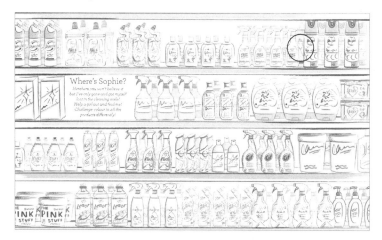

Help Sophie! Page 193

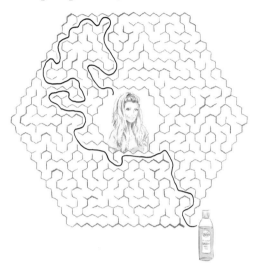

Word Scramble Page 219

1. chin hilts .... hinchlist
2. ad puffin sherry .... fresh'n up friday
3. hila hnuch .... hinch haul
4. mewls tax .... wax melts
5. air nan .... narnia
6. chin hams .... hinchmas
7. lowibse leverages .... elvis elbow grease
8. hartshorn shake .... sharon the shark
9. elsy grog grove .... gregory gloves
10. achiest blob .... cloth babies

Sudoku Fun 2 Page 224

8	6	7	2	1	3	9	5	4
4	1	2	5	7	9	6	8	3
9	5	3	4	6	8	7	2	1
1	7	9	3	5	4	8	6	2
6	3	8	1	2	7	4	9	5
5	2	4	9	8	6	1	3	7
2	9	5	6	4	1	3	7	8
3	8	1	7	9	5	2	4	6
7	4	6	8	3	2	5	1	9

Where's Henry? Pages 220–221

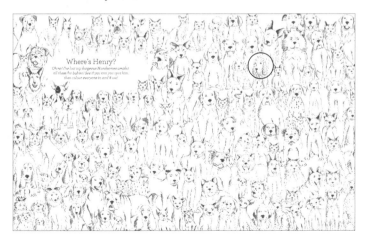

Completed Dot-To-Dot Page 244

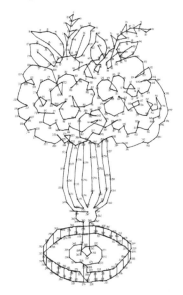

Help Henry! Page 255

Hinching Tools Word Search Page 245

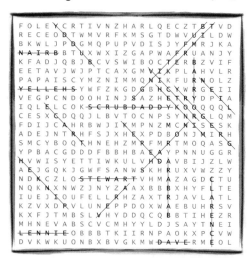

Derek; Buff Tings; Pinkeh; Minkeh; Barry; Kermit; Neil; Gregory; Shelley; Sharon; Stewart; Buddy; Brian; Barbara; Vera; Trace; Victor; Scrub Daddy; Dave; Clarence; Lennie

Hinch Your Sudoku Page 268